THE COMPLETE STORY

Other Titles in the Crowood MotoClassic Series

THE COMPLETE STORY

MATTHEW VALE

THE CROWOOD PRESS

First published in 2011 by
The Crowood Press Ltd
Ramsbury, Marlborough
Wiltshire SN8 2HR

www.crowood.com

British Library Cataloguing-in-Publication Data
A catalogue record for this book is available from the British Library.

ISBN978 1 84797 238 5

Designed, typeset and edited by Focus Publishing,
Sevenoaks, Kent

Printed and bound in Singapore by Craft Print International Ltd

Contents

Preface

The Norton Commando rose from the ashes of the defunct Associated Motor Cycles (AMC), which was placed into receivership in August 1966. After its failure, AMC, which comprised the well-known makes of AJS, Matchless, Norton, Francis-Barnett and James, was bought by Dennis Poore's Manganese Bronze Holdings, an industrial conglomerate that already had some motorcycle interests as it owned Villiers, the two-stroke engine manufacturers. After the purchase AMC continued to trade as Norton Matchless, and the new company produced an assortment of stopgap Norton and Matchless bikes that kept the Norton name alive. However, a new model was needed quickly if the company were to survive and the 750cc Commando was the result. The Commando was launched in 1967 when prototypes were shown at that year's London Motorcycle Show at Earl's Court. The bike was a 750cc Norton Atlas engine rehoused in a new frame and would be sold under the Norton Villiers banner, with Matchless consigned to history.

The Norton Commando, along with the Triumph and BSA triples, was one of the British motorcycle industry's last innovative products before the Japanese tsunami swept the old factories away. The Commando was born out of dire necessity – a new model in the Norton range was long overdue – and with clever use of existing and new technology it put to bed one of the biggest bugbears of British bikes: vibration. But the Commando was more than just a rehash of old technology: it also embraced the new tool of marketing and exploited the concept of modular design.

Put into production in 1968, the Commando, as the first new product of the Norton Villiers organization, was marketed extensively to enhance the company's image and to try to move the British motorcycle industry into the 1970s. With modern styling and an innovative anti-vibration system, the Commando was an immediate success and was 'Machine of the Year' in *Motor Cycle News* for five years running (1968–72).

A modular design concept was used to the maximum to enable the bike to fill every niche market possible while making minimal changes to the product. When introduced to the public the Commando's radical Wolff-Olins styling and revolutionary rubber-mounted engine and transmission caused a major stir in the market. During its relatively short production run the Commando could be had as a 'standard' roadster, a sports bike, an out-and-out production racer, long-distance tourer, a café racer, a chopper and a street scrambler – all achieved through the judicious mix and matching of tanks, exhausts, handlebars, fairings and seats, while the core engine, frame and running gear remained the same. Despite these innovations the Commando, like the rest of the British bike industry, was unable to compete with the flood of high-quality bikes from Japanese manufacturers: production stalled in 1975 and eventually spluttered to a halt in 1977. More than three decades later, however, the Commando still has a strong following in the classic bike market, with a number of specialist companies addressing the worldwide market for spares and repairs, and, with just about 100 per cent spares availability, new bikes are still available to order.

This book documents the Commando's main technical features and development history, and identifies the models that made up the range, from the first 20M3 and Fastback to the final batch of electric start Mark 3s. The rider's view is catered for with interviews with present and former owners, details of the technical improvements and fixes that have been developed over the years are given, and the complete restoration of a 1971 model is documented.

Acknowledgements

This is my fifth book and I would like to thank all those who helped me in writing it, including: My wife Julia, daughter Lizzie and father-in-law Ed, for their encouragement and putting up with me disappearing into the garage or study!

Wally Olins, for meeting me and describing the process and thoughts that went into Wolff Olins's work on the Commando, and to Norman White for taking time to tell me about the performance shop and the racing Nortons.

Frank Westworth and Rowena Hoseason of *RealClassic* magazine, who supplied many of the photographs used in this book and gave me much encouragement during my rebuild, and for Frank's mirth at the Hi-riding result.

Neil McCallum of Triples Workshop of Wakefield, who not only sourced the bike restored in the book, but also supplied pictures of his 'SS' model.

Keith Glassborrow, Pete Isted, Les Ward, Ken Rawlinson and Tony Sumner, for their anecdotes, reminiscences, pictures and memories of owning and riding their Commandos.

The *RealClassic* message board members (you know who you are!) and the Jerry Doe Norton Commando website members for their advice, guidance and support.

David Thomas of Hume, Virginia, USA, for the pictures of his 1969 'S' type 'in the day' and of his battery carrier and oil tank assemblies, and to Peter Sakai and Frank Charriaut for the pictures of the Ron Wood Flat Tracker, all contacted through Jerry Doe's Access Norton website, www.jerrydoe.com

This book is dedicated to the memory of Edmund Charles Humfryes, father-in-law and friend, who passed away on 19 June 2010.

1 Prelude and Overview

The Norton Commando was introduced to the world and the British public at the annual Earl's Court Motorcycle Show in London in September 1967. The new model's combination of innovative engineering and startling styling gave it a great deal of publicity, but the bike had a lot to live up to. The Japanese were making inroads into the worldwide motorcycle markets previously dominated by the British industry: by the mid-1960s the UK market for small bikes was completely dominated by the Japanese and Honda was breaking into the big bike market with their 450cc CB450 'Black Bomber'. Even though they were larger and had more performance, the offerings from Norton Villiers were looking distinctly lacklustre in comparison to the well-engineered and well-equipped bikes from the East. Market intelligence was beginning to hear whispers about even bigger Japanese bikes – eventually realized with the launch of Honda's 750cc 4-cylinder superbike in 1969 In addition, the ever increasing power output of Norton's 360-degree parallel twins was causing their vibration to increase to levels that were affecting mechanical reliability and rider comfort. Rumours were also starting to circulate about a new multiple cylinder market-leading bike from Norton's British rival, the huge BSA/Triumph group, to replace the venerable 650cc twin-cylinder Bonneville and A65. As with the Honda, the BSA/Triumph offering was to displace 750cc, but would have three cylinders: a configuration that would still greatly reduce vibration in comparison to the big twins in the range.

The one area in which the British bikes were ahead of the Japanese offerings was in handling and road holding, and the reputation of Norton's race-bred Featherbed frame was second to none. However, Norton Villiers management knew that they could no longer afford to follow the cheap

The prototype Commando was pretty similar to the production model, but was painted in space age silver all over with an orange seat.

Clive Vandervell, whose grandfather Charles owned Nortons until the 1950s, shows off a Norton apprentice-built model of the Norton Model 7, which was the first application of the engine that would eventually power the Commando.

and traditional British industry route of simply updating the existing range with some minor improvements and new colours – the Japanese had educated the market to expect much more sophistication in motorbike design, along with change and innovation – and so a major break with the old order was needed. While the Featherbed frame would be a hard act to follow, Norton Villiers realized that a completely new motorbike was needed and Dennis Poore, the Norton Villiers chairman, ordered the design team to start development of just such a machine in 1966, with a target launch date of the Earl's Court Motorcycle Show in September 1967. This was achieved with the Commando, which sported a new frame and reused the existing Nor-

ton 750cc motor. The styling of the bike was carried out by Wolff Olins, a design consultancy, and was completely unlike what had gone before, with an integrated look that has now achieved classic status. The bike was introduced to the public at the Earl's Court show in September 1967 and was just what the British public had been waiting for.

The Commando would go on from this good start to be incredibly successful. Featuring the power characteristics and handling of a big traditional British twin, but as vibration-free as a Japanese 4-cylinder bike, it offered a unique combination of features that resulted in it being *Motor Cycle News*'s 'Machine of the Year' for five years running (1968–72). During its production

*The final production Commando, the 850 Mark 3, featured electric start, disc brakes front
and rear (the front is uprated on this example), and lots of other detail improvements.*

run Norton was able to create a wide variety of sporting, road and touring models simply by changing seat, fuel tanks and exhaust systems, giving a flexible and economical way of addressing the various niches that made up the motorcycle market at the time.

Time was to run out for Norton and the Commando, however, and production ceased in 1977 with a final run of the Mark 3 models after Norton Villiers Triumph had been placed into liquidation.

Norton Commando: The Background

Norton was originally formed in 1898 by James Lansdowne Norton as the Norton Manufacturing Company to supply cycle components. The company produced its first powered two-wheeler in 1902, equipped with a proprietary 143cc Clement engine, and started producing bikes with the Norton name on the tank in 1904. In 1913 the company went into liquidation and was bought by the owner of the firm that did much of Norton's machining work, R. T. Shelley Ltd, which in turn was owned by C. A. Vandervell & Co. Under this new ownership, Norton went on to have a long and glorious history producing road and racing motorbikes throughout the first half of the twentieth century. In the early 1950s

the chairman, Charles Anthony Vandervell, who was then eighty-one years old, decided to capitalize on the company's successful record, both commercially and on the track, by floating Norton and the subsidiary company of R. T. Shelley on the London Stock Exchange to help alleviate the effects of the death duties that would be imposed on his estate by the British government on his demise.

The majority shareholder following a successful floatation in February 1953 was Associated Motor Cycles (AMC), who produced AJS, Matchless, James and Francis-Barnett motorbikes. AMC allowed Norton to continue to operate largely independently, although various components were shared between the different model ranges. In September 1966 the AMC group was bought by Manganese Bronze Holdings, the chairman of which was the industrialist Dennis Poore. Part of Manganese Bronze's industrial empire included Villiers, the famous maker of two-stroke engines for motorbikes and other applications, and with the acquisition of AMC, Norton Villiers was formed to take on all the group's motorcycle activities.

By 1966 the main four-stroke engine powering the AMC range was Norton's 750cc Atlas unit. Both this and the 650cc version were

The Norton 750cc motor was first seen in the Featherbed-framed Atlas. It was a 360-degree vertical twin, with pushrod-operated valves.

The Atlas had a pressed steel chain case. This was a source of oil leaks and was replaced with an alloy unit on the Commando.

The unified twin featured unit construction, with the engine and gearbox cased in a single set of castings. It was more modern than the Atlas pre-unit engine, but never made it into production.

The unified twin engine unit was compact and clean, with neatly integrated gearbox. The barrel was deeply spigotted into the cases.

The unified twin featured a neat alloy primary chain case and fitted well into the Featherbed frame.

developments of the 500cc Dominator unit, originally designed by Bert Hopwood in the 1940s and first seen in 1949 in the plunger framed Model 7. Norton had already made two attempts to replace this engine. In the late 1950s they designed a twin-cylinder 650cc pushrod operated overhead valve engine that was of unit construction (with the engine, primary drive and gearbox incorporated in a single set of casings), known as the 'unified twin'. While a couple of engines, and, it was rumoured, a Featherbed framed running prototype were produced, this project was abandoned in the early 1960s following the AMC takeover of Norton and AMC's dire financial position before all the problems were ironed out. A running engine was placed in a Featherbed rolling chassis by a member of the Norton Owners Club in the UK.

A further project, aimed at replacing the 750cc Atlas-engined machines in the AMC range, was the P10, a double overhead cam unit construction twin. This was designed by Charles Udall of Velocette fame when he joined AMC in 1961 and was being developed for production when AMC failed in mid-1966. The motor was originally 650cc and was stretched to 785cc for the new project, but problems arose during its development. The P10's twin overhead cams were driven by a very long chain encased in three tubes, two running up the timing side to the head in a 'V', giving the engine a slight resemblance to a Vincent Comet, and the third running across the top of the cylinder head between the two cam covers. The engine was housed in a new frame using standard Norton 'Roadholder' forks and swinging arm rear suspension. The prototype engine, dubbed the P800, was mechanically noisy, however, with much of the racket coming from the excessively long cam chain, and there were issues regarding the ease of assembly for production, oil leaks and a lack of power: the venerable Atlas unit could produce comparable power with a bit of tweaking by Norton engine man Bob Wyatt.

When Manganese Bronze took over AMC in 1966 there was no coherent strategy to take the company forward, and the development of a much needed new flagship engine had stalled.

The P10 engine was placed into a Featherbed frame to form the prototype P800.

New impetus was needed and Dennis Poore reacted by appointing Dr Stefan Bauer as Director of Engineering, backed up by a team of engineers with solid motorcycling experience. The intention was that Dr Bauer, who came from Rolls-Royce and had also worked in the atomic industry, would bring in ideas from outside the motorcycle industry and would oversee the design of an all new motor cycle that could then be developed into a production machine by the experienced motorcycle engineers in his team. The team comprised designers Bernard Hooper and John Favill, along with Charles Udall, the Chief Designer at AMC's Woolwich works, draughtsman Tony Denniss and Wally Wyatt in charge of experimental work. Bob Trigg joined the organization in February 1967 to take overall charge of the design. The target set by Dennis Poore was to introduce a viable prototype to the public at the Earl's Court Motorcycle Show in September 1967 and have a machine in production for the 1968 season.

Development of the Commando

Dr Bauer took on board the need to understand his new role. When he rode pillion on some existing twins, he was shocked by the level of vibration and discomfort he experienced and he determined that the new bike must isolate the rider from the inevitable vibration of a parallel twin. He also disliked the Featherbed frame from an engineering point of view and quickly put together the design that would become the Commando frame: a large diameter top tube to provide torsional rigidity between the steering head and the swinging arm, with lightweight, non-load bearing tubular structures to support the engine and rider. The machine was to be completely new – or at least new to the public, since the basis of the design was initially to be the P10 engine.

The P10 engine underwent an intensive redesign by Tony Denniss, Bernard Hooper and

The P10 engine was intended to form the basis of an Atlas replacement, but too many problems led to it being abandoned. The length of the cam chain can be appreciated from this side view.

John Favill that resulted in the engine being changed so much it was redesignated Z26. The redesign was comprehensive, with the head, bottom end and gearbox all being modified, but problems with vibration, power output and the difficulty of assembling the engine in a production environment persisted. The design team was rapidly running out of time to meet Poore's deadline and they were eventually forced to go back to the drawing board and come up with a viable way of using the existing Atlas engine. With a mere eleven weeks before the Earl's Court show, and with money running out, the team worked frantically to design the bike that would become the Commando using the existing 750cc Norton engine. Rubber mounts were incorporated to isolate the rider from the Atlas unit's vibration, but the apparently insurmountable problem was keeping the rear chain on its sprockets: with rubber mounting the pull of the chain and the movement of the engine could shift the gearbox out of line with the rear wheel, leading to the chain jumping off the sprockets. The breakthrough came when Hooper and Trigg worked out that by isolating the engine, gearbox and swinging arm (and hence the rear wheel), and rigidly joining them together, the rear chain line could be kept constant.

The main issue then was to preserve the handling by making sure the front and rear wheels were kept in line. This was done by limiting the movement of the rubber-mounted unit to the vertical plane, so that the engine, gearbox and swinging arm could go up and down, but not move from side to side. This kept the wheels in line and preserved the handling. The arrangement also meant that Dr Bauer's new lightweight frame could be used as it did not need to be heavily built to absorb the engine vibration, thus saving weight. The Commando with its unique Isolastic rubber mounting system was born. The Commando frame had a tough act to follow and acquitted itself well against the reputation held by the Featherbed. All the contemporary road tests found the Commando handled and steered well, but there was always a slight reluctance to say it was as good as the Featherbed.

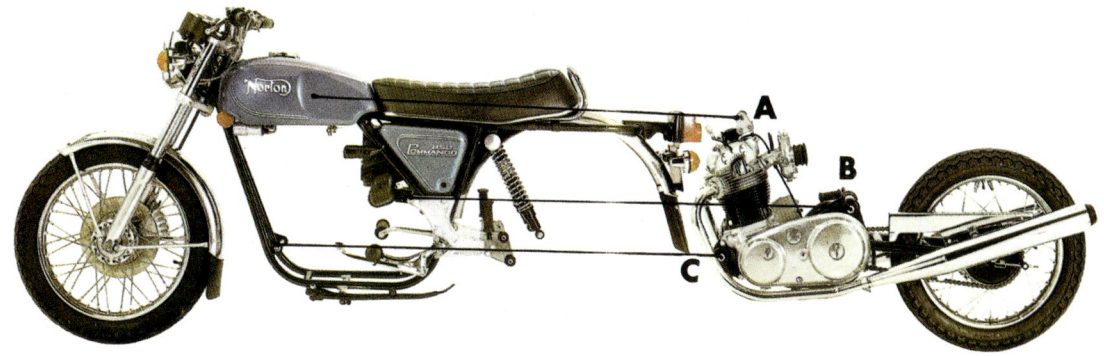

The Isolastic system isolated the engine from the rider and, by rigidly connecting it to the gearbox and swinging arm, kept the chain in alignment.

Commando Branding and Marketing

One particular aspect of the Commando that marked it out from the mainstream British bikes of the time was its marketing. At the time the concepts of marketing and, especially, branding were new and Norton was probably the first motorcycle manufacturer to adopt modern practices: it was certainly the first British manufacturer to do so. As the launch of the Commando approached Dennis Poore instigated a project to style and market the bike in a manner that would give it a unique identity and place in the market. One of Dennis Poore's relations knew Wally Olins, who had formed the Wolff Olins agency with Michael Wolff. Wolff Olins pitched for the project and won: when interviewed by the author, Wally Olins observed somewhat wryly that there were several (about six) people within Norton Villiers overseeing the project – more than Wolff Olins had working on it.

The overall design of the bike was already laid out when the project was started, and Norton supplied Wolff Olins with a single prototype for them to work on. Michael Wolff and Wally Olins concentrated on the branding elements of the brief, while team member David Bristow worked on the bike at Wolff Olins's north London premises at 81 Parkway, Camden, to translate the branding work into reality. These premises were so small that any work on the bike had to be done outside in the street, and the bike had to be covered up with a groundsheet when it rained. Wally Olins wondered at the time if this was how the Japanese companies carried out their model development!

Brand awareness was not part of the brief – mainly because the concept of 'brand' as we know it today did not exist in the late 1960s. What Wolff Olins did was probably the first attempt to create a new 'brand' for an automotive product. The original concept was that the bike needed to be different from what had gone before and what was then on the market. While much is made of the prototype's finish of overall silver and an orange seat, the plan was for the production machines to retain the overall silver finish but for the models within the range to be differentiated by the use of vibrant seat colours. This idea was picked up by Suzuki in the late 1970s and early '80s with their Katana models, in which the seat colour was an important element in the overall design and was used for model designation. Many of today's bikes use the colour of the saddle as an integral element of the styling, rather than using an overall black finish or, if you were lucky, a grey top, as was the norm in the 1960s and into the '70s.

One vital element of the design was the use of the 'Green Dot' to define the brand. This was both simple and powerful. It was devised by Michael Wolff and was used to link all the disparate elements of the proposed brand together. Wolff Olins thought up numerous applications for the Green Dot to reinforce the Norton brand, including using green balloons at race meetings above the

NORTON COMMANDO 750

The infamous Green Blob formed part of the Wolff Olins team's branding exercise. It survived to become the Andover Norton Green Globe trademark, still in use today.

The 1968 production Commando remained faithful to the Wolff Olins-styled original.

Norton pits, producing green 45rpm records with recordings of Stefan Bauer talking about the bike in the factory at Plumstead above the sound of engines running, producing simple round Green Dot lapel badges and of course the Green Dot on the prototype's fuel tank and instruments where convention said the factory name should be. Originally it was proposed that the Norton Villiers name was not placed on the bike at all, but the factory insisted on having a second round badge with 'Norton Villiers' written on it in block script above a traditional 'Norton' logo.

This was a small example of how the Norton Villiers management did not get the concept of branding. While Dennis Poore was enthusiastic and understood the concept, the old guard were not so keen. The use of the Green Dot as a brand identifier was not understood and was ridiculed by some elements in Norton Villiers. The Wolff Olins team had a terrible time trying to persuade the Norton Villiers management to 'brand'. Wolff Olins, for example, suggested they sell motorcycle gloves with the Green Dot on them, only to be told that Norton Villiers was a motorcycle factory and did not make clothes. Trying a different slant,

when the factory secured an order for modified Commandos from the Paris Police, Wally suggested that they produce a limited edition 'Paris Police' version aimed at the US West Coast market and back it up with associated helmets, leather jackets and other items to cash in on the glamour and style of the French machines. This suggestion was met with a complete lack of understanding – the factory basically said these are French machines; we cannot sell them to the US! Despite these issues and difficulties, the bike caused a sensation when it was first displayed at the 1967 London Motorcycle Show, and a very favourable response was had from the press – albeit showing an unhealthy obsession with the orange seat and the green blob!

The press also tended to miss the point of the branding exercise. In its review of the Earl's Court Show, *Motorcycle Sport* was somewhat puzzled:

The strangest thing of all – there were no Norton Villiers tank motifs, just a large, saucer shaped green blob of plastic on the tank side. There were mysterious pale green discs all over the stand. Was it some subtle form of subliminal advertising or recognition signs for little green men from outer space?

So they almost got the idea, but remember that all this occurred in the late 1960s, a few years before the emergence of branding on clothing and accessories (and complete bikes) in the early 1970s with Honda's 'Hondastyle', Texaco Heron Team Suzuki and of course Norton's own John Player Norton brand. These early attempts at branding pale into insignificance when you look at today's market, where companies recognize their brand and its value – witness the wide range of accessories and lifestyle items produced by companies such as Triumph and Harley-Davidson. Rumour has it that Harley makes more from its franchising activities than it makes from selling bikes.

The prototype bike was also displayed by Wolff Olins at the British Design Show in New York, where it again generated huge publicity.

Wally feels today that the project could have been so much better, since Wolff Olins was a young and inexperienced company that had some excellent ideas but lacked the experience to drive them through to fruition. The project also suffered from the Commando not being properly developed as a machine because the Norton Villiers management did not put enough money behind the development of the product and they remained ignorant of the concepts of branding. Wally disparagingly says that he looks on the project as his contribution to the demise of the British motorcycle industry, but the author thinks that the adoption of several of Wolff Olins's ideas in the product and the publicity generated by that iconic prototype may have actually helped to keep the flickering embers of the British bike industry burning (or at least smoking) for a few more years.

While the branding strategy proposed by Wolff Olins was not taken up with any great consistency by Norton, the Green Dot did develop into a green globe and appeared on the early Commando-specific literature and in advertisements for the bike. The adverts and brochures that had the most appeal to the customers of the time, however, featured the traditional selling method for motorcycles – drape an attractive female over the bike and the sales will follow. The advertising produced for the Commando in the early 1970s included classics of the genre that are still regarded with affection today.

Into Production

The first Commandos were produced at the old AMC works at Plumstead Road in south-east London, an area that was scheduled for redevelopment, and government grants were available to organizations that were prepared to move to designated 'growth areas'. Norton Villiers took advantage of this government largesse and chose to relocate the manufacturing of the Commando to Andover in rural Hampshire, some 100 miles west of London. The site was close to Thruxton airfield, which also hosted the famous race circuit at which the Norton AJS Competition and Development Department was based. However, the operation in Andover was essentially that of assembling the bikes, as the engines and gearboxes were manufactured at the large Villiers works in Wolverhampton in the Midlands and the frames were made by Reynolds in Birmingham. These were then trucked down to Andover overnight. Completed bikes would then be trucked back up to the Norton Villiers distribution organization in the Midlands. Production stated in Andover in the first part of 1971 and the transport-intensive operation continued for some eighteen months until full production was shifted to the Villiers works in Wolverhampton in 1973. The main Andover site was turned over to spares distribution and storage, but the competition department remained at the Thruxton circuit. With the takeover of Triumph in 1973, Norton Villiers Triumph (NVT) was formed, but with continued financial problems, NVT was forced into liquidation in August 1975. This meant a controlled run-down of the Wolverhampton factory and the tailing off of Commando production. With the emergence of NVT Engineering from the ashes of NVT, a batch of 500 Commandos was completed at Wolverhampton between June and September 1976. This was followed by a batch of 1500 Commandos produced at Wolverhampton and completed by September 1977, and in 1978 a final small batch of Commandos was produced or assembled at Andover. In the third volume of his *British Motor Cycles since 1950* (Patrick Stephens Ltd, 1986), Steve Wilson claims that this final batch comprised thirty bikes. So production of the Commando finally ceased, having moved from Plumstead to Andover, to Wolverhampton and then back to Andover.

2 Model Development

After its public unveiling at the September 1967 Earl's Court show, Norton had less than a year to get the bike into production and on the market. The first true production model hit the streets in March 1968, with most going to the USA; the bike was available to the buying public in the UK in May 1969, just in time for the summer season. Initially the bike was only produced in Fastback form, although the name had not then been coined, and was styled virtually the same as the prototype seen the previous year. The bike sported the Atlas-based 750cc motor, the Norton four-speed gearbox and a new diaphragm spring clutch: these features would remain broadly the same for the life of the model, although the engine capacity would grow to 828cc. The bike

used Bauer's spine frame and the Isolastic engine mounting system. The main difference from the prototype was in the finish, which retreated from the 'space age' overall silver and orange seat finish to a more practical and traditional black frame, black seat, and conventionally painted tank and seat tail in red, green or silver. The oil tank and side panel retained the silver finish to give a still striking look to the new model.

The Commando range was later expanded to cover most of the niche markets that made up the big bike market at the time. Norton approached the need to address several niche markets with what was essentially a single model range in a way that differed from that adopted by the rival Triumph and BSA concerns. The Commando was

The first production Commando was the Fastback model, with a striking rear tail that gave the bike a sleek appearance.

The Fastback is still popular today. Here is one of Les Emery's 1000cc bikes alongside an original specification machine.

the only bike in Norton's range by 1969 (the Featherbed framed 650cc Mercury was produced in limited numbers alongside the Commando in 1968), and the company's strategy was to cover as many niche markets as possible using the same basic mechanical components (engine, gearbox, frame, wheels and forks) and changing peripheral parts, such as fuel tank, seat, exhaust system and handlebars. This gave individual models their own character and made them easily distinguishable, giving the market the impression of a bigger range of bikes. This was in contrast to the approach adopted by BSA and Triumph, where the mechanics of the various models differed – single and twin carburettors for the Trophy and Bonneville, for example, along with higher or lower compression ratios and different camshafts. There was less alteration of the cycle parts in the BSA and Triumph bikes: while the frames tended to be the same, fuel tank capacity, front brake sizes and paint finishes differed between models.

This minimal change approach served Norton well. Although some models were short-lived, the range managed to cover most of the big bike market niches throughout the years, from rip-roaring road burner to custom chopper to big tourer. Importantly, the policy allowed Norton to introduce new models with a minimum of changes to the fundamental bike, and this limited disruption to the production line and helped to keep the spares inventory at a minimum.

The table on page 22 shows the Commando models produced year by year, and shows the start and finish dates for production where they are known. The Commando models were given Mark numbers by the factory, but these were not used in the marketing material or the workshop and parts manuals, so are generally not very well known. In general the Mark numbers apply to a model year and when used were common across the models that made up a particular year. However, some models never had a Mark number

Model Specifications

	1969 Fastback	1971 Roadster
Engine capacity	745cc/45 cu in	745cc/45 cu in
Bore/stroke (mm)	73 × 89	73 × 89
Compression ratio	8.9:1	9:1
Claimed power	60bhp at 6800	60bhp at 6800
Carburettors	30mm	30mm
Gearbox sprocket and ratio: top	19 tooth 4.84:1 21 tooth 4.35:1	19 tooth 4.84:1
Gearbox sprocket and ratio: third	19 tooth 5.9:1 21 tooth 5.35:1	19 tooth 5.9:1
Gearbox sprocket and ratio: second	19 tooth 8.25:1 21 tooth 7.42:1	19 tooth 8.25:1
Gearbox sprocket and ratio: first	19 tooth 12.4:1 21 tooth 11.18:1	19 tooth 12.4:1
Tyres: front	3.00 ×19	4.10 × 19
Tyres: rear	3.50 or 4.00 × 19	4.10 × 19
Front brake (in/cm)	TLS 8/20.3 drum	TLS 8/20.3 drum
Rear brake (in/cm)	SLS 7/17.8 drum	SLS 7/17.8 drum
Petrol tank capacity (UK gals/US gals/litres)	3.25/3.9/15	2.25/2.7/10.2
Oil tank capacity (UK pints/US pints/litres)	5/6/2.9	5/6/2.9
Seat height in/cm	31/79	31/79
Wheelbase in/cm	56.75/144.2	56.75/144.2
Ground clearance in/cm	6/15.24	6/15.24
Weight lb/kg	395/179	385/175

assigned, and some models missed out on some Mark numbers: for example, the SS should be a Mark 3 but was never named as such, and the first 750 Interstate was a Mark 4 (there was no Mark 1, 2 or 3).

Commando 750cc 20M3 and Fastback: 1968–73

The first production Commando was designated Model 20M3 (believed to stand for 'Model 20 Mark 3' – the Atlas was the Model 20) and was introduced to the public in April 1968. The bike was very similar to the prototype shown at Earl's Court the previous September, but the finish was toned down. The all-silver finish and orange seat of the prototype were discarded, with a traditional and more practical black frame and seat substituted, but the overall styling of the prototype was retained.

The innovative rear seat fairing and the two 'ears' at the front of the seat gave the Commando a new and modern appearance, while the toned-down colour scheme made the bike more acceptable to the relatively conservative buyer. Early tailpieces carried a round silver badge, with

1972 Interstate Combat	1973 Mk1 850 Roadster	1975 850 Mk 3 Interstate
745cc/45 cu in	828cc/55 cu in	828cc / 55 cu in
73 × 89	77 × 89	77 × 89
10:1	8.5:1	8.5:1
65bhp at 6500	60bhp at 5900	58bhp at 5900
32mm	32mm	32mm
19 tooth 4.84:1; 20 tooth 4.6:1; 21 tooth 4.35:1	21 tooth 4.38:1	20 tooth 4.6:1 22 tooth 4.185:1
19 tooth 5.9:1; 20 tooth 5.6:1; 21 tooth 5.35:1;	21 tooth 5.3:1	20 tooth 5.57:1 22 tooth 5.1:1
19 tooth 8.25:1; 20 tooth 7.8:1; 21 tooth 7.42:1	21 tooth 7.45:1	20 tooth 7.83:1 22 tooth 6.84:1
19 tooth 12.4:1; 20 tooth 11.8:1; 21 tooth 11.18:1	21 tooth 11.2:1	20 tooth 11.79:1 22 tooth 10.71:1
4.10 × 19	4.10 × 19	4.10 × 19
4.10 × 19	4.10 × 19	4.10 × 19
TLS 8/20.3 drum	10.7/270mm disc	10.7/270mm disc
SLS 7/17.8 drum	SLS 7/17.8 drum	10.7/270mm disc
Glass fibre 5.2/6.25/23.6 Steel 5.4/6.5/24.6	2.25/2.7/10.2	5.25 / 4.8 / 23.9
5/6/2.9	5/6/2.9	5 / 6 / 2.9
31/79	31/79	31 / 79
56.75/144.2	56.75/144.2	56.75 / 144.2
6/15.24	6/15.24	6 / 15.24
395/179	418/191	430 / 195

the script 'Norton' below with 'Norton Villiers' in block capitals above it. The engine was a lightly modified Atlas unit, a 745cc vertical twin, with pushrod operated overhead valves, twin 30mm Amal Concentric carburettors and a separate four-speed gearbox. The forward stance of the engine, matching the angle of the front down tubes, along with the strong horizontal line created by the rear fairing, seat and fuel tank, gave the bike an identity unlike anything else on the market, but still recognizably a British big twin. The 3½ gal (3.9 US gal, 15ltr) fuel tank was made out of glass fibre, and carried the same round badge as was placed on either side of the tail fairing. The steel oil tank carried 5 imperial pints (6 US pints/2.9ltr) and was rubber mounted on the right-hand side of the frame, just behind the air filter, with the filler cap at the rear, accessible only after removing the seat. The seat was fixed using two slotted lugs that engaged in the rear shock absorber top mounts and was held in place by another Commando styling icon, the round alloy knurled nuts that could be undone by hand. There was no cover over the oil tank, which extended forward to the nose of the seat ears, and the left-hand side had a glass fibre cover for the

Commando Models

Model Year:	1967	1968	1969	1970	1971	1972	1973	1974	1975	1976	1977
750cc Models											
Prototypes	Sept Earl's Court Show										
20MS – 750 Commando		International Feb									
Fastback			March	Sept Mk 2	Jan Mk 3	Jan Mk 4	Feb Mk 5				
Fastback LR					June	Jan Mk 4	Feb Mk 5				
'R'			March to mid-1969								
'S' Type			March	End June							
SS					May–Sept						
Roadster				March Mk 2	Mk 3	Jan Mk 4	Mk 5				
Interstate						Introduced Jan Mk 4	Mk 5				
Interpol				March Mk 2	Mk 3	Mk 4	Mk 5				
Hi-Rider					May Mk 3	Jan Mk 4	Mk 5				
Norvil Production Racer				Introduced	Production	End of production					
Short Stroke 750							Limited number produced, both engines only and complete bikes				
850cc Models											
Roadster							April Mk 1 Sept Mk 1a	Mk 2/Mk 2a	March Mk 3	Mk 3	End Oct Mk 3
Interstate							April Mk 1 Sept Mk 1a	Mk 2/Mk 2a	March Mk 3	Mk 3	End Oct Mk 3
JPN								April	End Feb		
Interpol							April Mk 1 Sept Mk 1a	Mk 2	Mk 3		End Oct Mk 3
Hi Rider							April Mk 1 Sept Mk 1a	Mk 2/Mk 2a	Mk 3		

The 1969 Fastback remained broadly the same as the launch machine. Note the Atlas-style silencers and rev counter drive from the timing side cover.

The Fastback makes a good tourer. The seat, with its distinctive ears flowing forwards into the tank, emphasizes the line of the side panel.

The Commando 'architecture' remained unchanged. Here is an early Fastback, showing the pre-1972 engine breather and Fastback side panels.

The alloy chain case has a single central fitting. A rubber band sits in a groove between the inner and outer faces to make the case pretty much oil tight.

The final fastback of 1972 had the roadster's upswept exhaust pipes and peashooters.

battery and toolkit that matched the shape of the oil tank. The fuel tank and rear seat fairing were coloured red, green or silver and the side panel and oil tank were finished in silver. The front mudguard was chromed, while the rear mud-guard was painted black to emphasize the lines of the rear seat tail fairing and was bolted to the bottom rear of the number plate. The chromed exhaust system comprised separate pipes, one for each cylinder, and large Atlas-style silencers running parallel to the ground on each side, rubber mounted to the alloy 'Z' plates. The instruments comprised a speedometer and tachometer and were housed on the traditional Commando alloy pods, which were bolted in position by the fork top nuts. The speedo did not have a trip function, only a milometer, and both instruments carried the solid green globe emblem – the only instance of the branding exercise to make it onto the production bike. The 7in chrome headlamp was mounted on black painted ears and carried an ammeter, light switch and blue main beam warning light. Two anachronisms were carried over from the Atlas: the external rev counter drive on the side of the timing cover (which initially did

not bear the cast 'Norton' script) and the points sitting at the rear inner edge of the timing cover where the magneto used to live. These were both old-fashioned features that seemed out of place with the bike's up-to-date image.

The mainly modern looks, however, were complemented by the Isolastic engine mounting system and together produced a machine that journalists of the day thought was exceptional: all the performance of a beefy British 750cc twin with none of the vibration that so often marred the riding experience. The punters agreed too, as was demonstrated when the Commando was voted 'Bike of the Year' in 1968 by the readers of the weekly Motor Cycle News (MCN). This feat was repeated for the following four years up to 1972, giving the Commando an unbroken run of five years.

The first official use of the 'Fastback' name came in March 1969, when the bike was named alongside the then new 'R' and 'S' types. The UK and US Fastback models differed little initially, the main alteration for the US market being high handlebars.

The year also saw the introduction of optional two-tone paintwork, with silver panels on each side of the fuel tank and the top of the rear fast-back moulding. The model adopted the repositioned contact breaker points in the timing cover and the new rev counter drive in the front of the crankcases in September 1969, some months after they first appeared on the 'S' type. The US market Fastback gained a Roadster-style exhaust system with upswept 'peashooter' silencers for 1970, giving the bike a more rakish look, while the more conservative UK market had to make do with the original Atlas style. At this time Norton repositioned the model as the 'two-wheeled Grand Tourer' of the range, as the Roadster had by now taken the fast street bike title.

The Fastback was still listed for sale in the US and UK up to the introduction of the Interstate in 1972, and finally disappeared at the end of the 1972 season.

Commando 750cc 'R' Type: 1969

The 'R' type was the first variant on the Commando. It was introduced in March 1969 but was destined to be one of the shorter-lived models. The model was essentially the forerunner to the Roadster model (from 1970) and was the first demonstration of the versatility of Norton's parts bin philosophy, being a lightly modified Fastback but having a completely different look as a result

of simply changing the fuel tank and seat; these parts would reappear on the more heavily modified 'S' type. The 'R' offered a sportier option to the road/touring biased Fastback and was described in an early 1969 US market brochure as:

> R Type Commando, Enduro Style. A rugged street scrambler with all the sports appeal of an Ascot flat-tracker.

This seemed a strange choice of words for what was a pure street bike, and really would be more appropriate for describing the later 'S' type. The 'R' type had the smaller 'S' type fuel tank, painted in red or blue with styling cutaways for the rider's knees and a Norton script decal on each side. This tank shape would evolve into the classic Roadster-style tank. The seat was conventionally styled, without the Fastback seat's 'ears' or rear fairing, and it followed the line of the rear mudguard, giving an upward tilt to the rear half. The seat cover was all black, with a pleated top and a chrome trim along the base. The front mudguard was identical to the Fastback's unit, while the rear mudguard was a traditional chromed unit, matching the front and replacing the black steel unit that lurked under the Fastback's rear tail moulding.

The 'R' type, here on the left next to a Fastback with the 1969 optional two tone paintwork, was the first variant of the Commando and intended as a US market bike.

*The 'R' type and the Fastback shared the high bars that the British
industry assumed was a prerequisite for US sales.*

*With its conventional fuel tank and seat the 'R' type was a more conservative
model and helped to widen the Commando's appeal.*

A separate glass fibre rear light carrier with round side reflectors was bolted to the rear mudguard and carried the number plate. The 'R' was fitted with a chrome headlamp, mounted on Fastback-style headlamp brackets in chrome rather than the 'S' type's chromed tube-type headlamp bracket. Other than these changes the model shared the rest of the Fastback's running gear and styling, with a low level exhaust system with cigar-type silencers running parallel to the ground.

The 'R' type also had the Fastback-style silver-painted oil tank on the right-hand side and a large matching silver-painted side panel on the left, although the 'R' type side panel (part number 06-1175) had some subtle differences to that listed for the Fastback (part number 06-0854) at the time. The 'R' type was discontinued in the middle of 1969 and was replaced by the Roadster model in 1970.

Commando 750cc 'S' Type: 1969–70

The Commando 'S' type was introduced after the 'R' type in 1969 and was the second variation on the Commando theme: an off-road styled 'Street Scrambler' version. The model complemented the road-oriented general purpose Fastback and was effectively a replacement for the Atlas-engined Norton Ranger/P11 range, the big off-roader in the AMC range, aimed at the US desert racer, which used the Norton engine in a Matchless G80CS scrambler-type frame. At the time, the 'Sport' label in the US related to off-road competition rather than the European road-racing idea, and so, with an eye to the large US market, Norton tailored this model to suit both the on-road 'Street Scrambler' market and the off-road 'Desert Sled' markets that were so popular in the USA.

The 'S' type had a high level off-road style exhaust system with both pipes running over the primary chain case on the drive side of the bike and connecting to two silencers, one above the other, suspended above the rear wheel axle. The system was the same in layout to that previously used on the Triumph TR6 and T100C Trophy systems. Norton's system used chrome-plated perforated steel heat shields on the pipes and twin reverse cone megaphone silencers: this was the first Commando to use the Norton 'peashooter' silencers.

The defining element of the 'S' type is the exhaust system.

The timing side of the 'S' type looks strangely bare without any exhaust pipes, but gives the bike a lean appearance.

The 'S' type pipes must have been a pipe bender's nightmare: the one on the timing side takes a convoluted route to cross over to the drive side.

From the rear the 'S' type presents a slim profile. The perforated heat shields were reasonably effective, but the rider's left leg still got warm.

The silencers were rubber mounted on a bracket that had its lower part fixed to the 'Z' plate and the upper to the frame. Moving away from the Fastback's unique styling, a new seat and a 2.25 gal (2.7 US gal/10.22ltr) glass fibre fuel tank were fitted. The seat was a conventional dual seat, without the Fastback's protruding ears or the glass fibre fairing at the rear, and this gave the whole bike a more traditional look, complemented by the 'R' type small tank with its 'Norton' script transfers and small knee indents. There were two glass fibre side panels, which were pared down with the front edge following the frame's bracing tubes to give an almost triangular shape. From then on this design was fitted to the 'Sports' versions of the Commando, with the larger, rectangular style being used on the tourers.

The ignition switch was carried in the front top corner of the drive side panel, with the key pointing outwards ready to snag the rider's leg. Behind the side panels a new oil tank sat across the frame, behind the standard air filter. Its filler cap was on the timing side as normal, but the oil feeds ran to and from the engine from the side of the front of the tank, and were clearly visible in front of the leading edge of the side panel. The battery slotted in across the frame, in a carrier mounted behind the oil tank. Traditional US-specification high and wide handlebars, a chromed 7 inch headlamp surrounded by and mounted on a circular chromed tube bracket, and a conventional chrome-plated rear mudguard finished off the look, which reflected the change in use that motor bikes were going through from practical forms of transport to lifestyle accessories where looks were more important than practicality. Importantly, the 'S' type received the stylish and practical repositioned contact breaker points in the timing cover, driven directly from the camshaft and the new rev-counter drive in the front of the crankcases. The new timing side outer case now had the 'Norton' script cast in.

The 'S' type was discontinued in June 1970, when its street scrambler role was taken over by the Roadster model and the off-road function was covered by the 'SS'.

A feature of the 'S' type was the chromed ring mount for the headlamp.

Not all 'S' types were yellow. Here is the 'S' type owned by Dave Thomas of Hume, Virginia, back in the early 1970s.

A custom paintjob marks out this early drum-braked Roadster.

The slim side panels on the Roadster help to reduce the bulk of the motor.

Commando 750cc Roadster: 1970–73

The Commando Roadster was the logical successor to the 'R' type. While it followed the same format, when introduced it was in fact based closely on the 'S' model rather than the Fastback-derived 'R'.

With its small fuel tank, which it shared with the previous year's 'R' model and the current 'S' model, abbreviated triangular 'S' type side panels, chromed front and rear mudguards, conventional dual seat with a kicked-up rear that followed the line of the mudguard, and a new low level exhaust system with upswept reverse cone megaphone silencers, the Roadster really defined the look that the fast road-oriented Commando would adopt for the rest of its life.

Like the 'R' before it, the Roadster shared a number of parts with the 'S' type: for 1970 these included the 'S' type headlamp surround and the 'S' type oil tank running across the frame with the battery mounted transversely behind it. The bike was designed for the urban rider, for whom its short range was more than compensated by the bike's good looks. With its attractive Roadster tank, colour-coded side panels and the upswept peashooter style silencers, which complemented and contrasted with the forward slope of the engine, the whole bike looked rakish and ready to go – and go fast.

The under-seat layout and headlamp treatment of all the model range was rationalized for 1971. The Roadster got the timing side full-length oil tank, which was fixed to the battery tray that held the battery fore and aft on the drive-hand side. The headlamp was mounted on a pair of conventional chromed brackets mounted on the fork stanchions between the yokes. The ignition switch was moved from the side panel to a bracket forward of the air cleaner, set in a two-part plastic pod that was still on the drive side.

For 1972 the roadster received the ill-fated Combat engine as an option, with all the attendant problems. The upside was that the twin leading shoe front brake was supplemented with the option of the new disc brake, which became a standard fitment later on in the model year. The 750 Roadster model carried on pretty much unchanged into the final 1973 model year.

The first 1970 Roadsters featured 'S' type headlamp mountings and a similar fuel tank, but the low exhaust pipes with upswept peashooter silencers were the Roadster trademark.

The Roadster tank was slim and had the fuel cap offset to the right, so it is possible to brim the tank with the bike on the side stand. Wide and high US bars look good and are comfortable up to illegal speeds.

The roadster was a lean and good-looking machine. Here is a 1972 model with black barrels signifying a Combat era engine and original front disc brake.

Fastback 750 LR (Long Range): 1971–73

The Commando LR (Long Range) was introduced in both the UK and US markets for the
1971 model year. As the name suggests, it was a
longer range version of the Commando.

The LR called on the experience gained in the
development of the Interpol, and used a modified
steel Interpol tank without the well for the radio
equipment. The new tank had a claimed capacity of 4 imp gal (4.7 US gal/18ltr), a useful
increase over the Fastback's 3.25 imp gal (3.9 US
gal/14.7ltr) and the Roadster's even smaller tank.

While the bike retained the Fastback-style rear
tailpiece, the seat lost the ears that wrapped round
the front of the tank. Otherwise the bike shared
the rest of its specification with the Fastback.

The model was effectively replaced by the
Interstate as the dedicated tourer in the range, but
soldiered on alongside the Interstate until the end
of the 750 models in 1973.

*The LR was a capable tourer
and had more conventional looks
and a longer range than the
Fastback.*

The LR tank was not as wide as that on the later Interstate and carried a useful 4 gal.

The LR model was basically a Fastback with a larger tank and new seat. The tank was the Interpol unit without the well for the radio. This one does not have the Fastback tailpiece.

Commando SS: 1971

The Commando SS or Street Scrambler variant, only produced between March and October 1971, was a replacement for the previous year's 'S' type. This Commando variant was probably one of the least likely to be used in anger, as it was supposed to be an off-road racer in the same mould as the Norton P11/Ranger or the Triumph Trophy. In the USA in the 1960s the big 650cc and 750cc twins from Triumph and Norton dominated the long-distance cross-country desert races. By 1971, however, the big four-stroke twins had had their day and this type of event was becoming the domain of the mid-capacity two-stroke single.

While the SS retained the Commando frame, which was most definitely designed for road use, the bike was fitted with all the off-road kit to give it the Street Scrambler look. This comprised high level exhaust pipes with peashooter silencers, set one each side, running over the top of the crankcase and gearbox. This gave good ground clearance and reflected the system fitted to some Norton P11 Scramblers. The front mudguard followed off-road styling and its mounting on the bottom fork yoke gave lots of clearance and a lower unsprung weight, while high and wide chrome handlebars with a motocross style bracing bar finished off the effect. A satin black, solid one-piece heat shield was mounted on each exhaust pipe, long enough to protect the rider and passenger's legs from the exhaust system, and a bash plate was fitted to protect the crankcases. A smaller 5¾in (14.6 cm) diameter chrome headlamp was fitted between standard headlamp brackets using longer 1in spacers. The 2gal fuel tank (2.3 US gal/9ltr) was the same as that used on the High-Rider model. The slim triangular side panels first seen on the 'R' type were fitted, finished in black and contrasting nicely with the Canary Yellow or Tangerine tank. It seemed to be a tradition for British factories to paint their US market off-road bikes bright yellow, allegedly because it meant that hunters in the woods could see the bike and not shoot it or the rider!

The SS did not last very long, since there were major problems with its exhaust system. The high level silencers were rubber mounted onto brackets fixed to the top of the rear frame tube, just behind the side panel below the top suspension mount, and contemporary road tests felt they stuck out too far, forcing the rider's leg to rest against them. Despite the rubber mounting, the exhaust pipes also tended to fracture at the exhaust port. These woes led to Norton recommending to dealers that they replace the high level pipes with a conventional Roadster set-up. The SS was only listed during 1971.

The Commando 750SS was sold as an on/off road machine. It sported high-level exhaust pipes and silencers, one on each side, a small headlamp and a 2 gal tank.

Neil McCallum's SS looks a treat with a single pipe each side, small headlamp and fuel tank and the high-level front mudguard.

Neil McCallum of Triples Workshops had a good-looking SS in stock in mid-2010. Apart from the seat and the 'S' type heat shields it is pretty much stock.

Commando 750 and 850 Hi-Rider: 1971–76

Introduced in May 1971, the Hi-Rider was Norton's take on the chopper culture that was (supposedly) sweeping the USA in the wake of the famous Peter Fonda and Dennis Hopper film *Easy Rider*. In the rapidly emerging Commando tradition it was a simple job to swap tank, seat, headlamp and handlebars to create a 'new' version of the bike, while retaining the underlying frame, engine, electrics and running gear. Norton made a selling feature of this in the 1975 US brochure, which claims that:

> ... the Hi-Rider provides its fans a welcome opportunity to enjoy the looks and comfort of a custom street machine without sacrificing the roadability of a Norton. With a Hi-Rider you just sit back, smile and keep on hangin' corners. No sweat.

Norton were even more cunning than usual with the design of the Hi-Rider, as they used the small chrome 5⅛in (14.6cm) diameter headlight assembly and the fuel tank from the SS model – bits that were already in the parts bin. The fuel tank was a small 2 gal (2.3 US gal/9ltr) capacity unit with a flip top filler cap centrally placed as far forwards as practical; if you squinted from certain angles it looked like a chopper-style 'peanut' tank.

The effect was not quite as good as it should have been, however, since the bottom line of the tank was straight, leaving the coils exposed to cooling air, but overall the unit looked the part and was available and proven. Slim triangular Roadster side panels complemented the tank to give a lean look. Leaving the tank aside, the defining elements of the styling were the handlebars and the seat. The handlebars were the classic Chopper style 37in (93cm) wide, 12¼in (31cm) rise Ape Hangers. These required longer cables for the clutch, brake and upper throttle and, on the post-1972 models with the disc brake, a longer hydraulic hose.

The seat had a chopperesque hump at its rear, with a chrome grab rail following the line of the hump and aping the styling of the 'sissy' bars that real choppers sported. The seat came in two versions. The first bikes had a short seat with little room between the rider and the hump, meaning that any pillion needed to be particularly friendly with the rider. The second version was introduced in 1972 as an option and was described as a dual seat. This seat retained the hump at the back, but was slightly longer than the original version to make life for pillions (and riders) a bit more comfortable.

The look was finished off with the 'SS' style 5½in headlamp, which again helped the bike to mimic the Chopper look without having extended forks; the unit was made by Lucas and was fixed in place using the standard headlight brackets rather than using a single bolt fixing to the bottom yoke, as was used on the classic Bates unit.

The Hi-Rider first appeared in 1971 in 750cc form, was retained in the 850cc range and remained listed right through to the final 850 Mark 3 model. For 1971 the tank and side panels were finished in Bright Yellow or Tangerine; this scheme was carried through to 1972. Black with gold lining was added to the options list for 1973, with the 1973 850 listed in black only. For 1974 Tangerine was the only listed colour. There has been some debate as to whether any Mark 3 versions were ever made, but the Hi-Rider seat, tank, 5½in headlamp and high handlebars (and associated cables and brake pipes) are all listed in the Mark 3 parts manual. A black and gold model also appears in the 1975 US brochure, but not in the UK brochure (nor is the model referenced in the UK brochure). The US brochure model is pictured being ridden on the road and it is not a studio mock-up, so it is certain that at least one Mark 3 model was built. As far as the author could discover, however, only a small number of Mark 3 Hi-Riders were actually built (one source puts it at between twenty and twenty-five), and since the 1975 parts book lists the Hi-Rider tank only in black with gold pinstripes, it is fairly certain that they were all in black.

The 1971 Commando featured in Chapter 6, restored as a Hi-Rider: note the RGM kick starter, which made it a lot easier to start.

The author's Hi-Rider shows the high bars and chopper seat. The bike is surprisingly pleasant to ride as long as you don't want to go too fast.

The Hi-Rider made it to the end of the line. Here is the brochure shot of the Mark 3 showing the longer 'dual' seat.

Commando 750 and 850 Interpol: 1970–77

The Norton Commando Interpol was the creation of Neil Shilton, who moved to Norton after successfully building up Triumph's police business with a range of machines that culminated in the 650cc Saint ('Stop Anything In No Time') model, a specially tuned and geared model designed to be extremely quick accelerating up to 100mph.

Norton had supplied bikes to the police in the past, notably the 750cc Atlas, but had never achieved the same level of sales as Triumph. The Commando as a bike was attractive to the police, as it offered greater performance and less vibration than Triumph's offerings. This gave a more comfortable time for the rider and was less destructive to the radio and other ancillary equipment. Poore was aware of this and employed Neil Shilton to produce a Commando-based police bike that became the Interpol. Shilton moved down to Andover in September 1969 and started developing the new model. The Interpol benefited from Norton's mix and match approach to models and simply needed changes to the seat, fuel tank and mudguards to produce the first version.

One problem was the fuel tank, since police forces were not keen on glass fibre tanks and insisted on using steel. Shilton commissioned the production of a new steel tank from Homers, based in Shirley, a suburb of Birmingham, that was based on the pressings used for the Featherbed-framed Atlas twins but with a new pressing for the underside to accommodate the Commando's frame spine. This tank could be had with or without a radio 'well' in the top: without the well, it formed the basis for the Fastback 'LR' tank.

Norton adopted the approach pioneered by Shilton at Triumph, where police forces could select a specification from a list of options rather than buying a basic bike and fitting the relevant equipment themselves. Norton went a step further by selling the bike direct to police forces. The Interpol was introduced in 1970 and the first sales were made to Sussex Police, who ordered seventeen machines that were delivered in March 1970.

The Interpol remained in production until the last Mark 3 models were produced, and provided a fine mount for police and other service users in many countries.

The first Interpols came with drum brakes, a steel tank based on the Atlas unit and a short single seat. Large mudguards protected the rider from road dirt.

Avon supplied the fairings for the Interpol.

The Interpol was fully faired and equipped for police duties. It was also supplied to the UK armed forces.

The final Interpols came in Mark 3 guise, complete with electric start.

Norvil Commando Production Racer: 1970–72

The Commando Production Racer was produced at Andover by the Norton Villiers Performance Shop (NVPS) between 1970 and 1972. The engines were very close in specification to the works Production racers being raced at the time. The only differences between the NVPS-built production racers sold to the general public and the factory-raced machines were intended to increase ground clearance and specifically to stop the primary chain case digging into the ground. This was achieved by repositioning the front Isolastic assembly by raising it ½in (9.5mm) and shifting it to the right by ½in (9.5mm), putting a chamfer on the bottom of the primary chain case and fitting a right-hand side exit for the exhaust system.

The engines of the PR bikes featured a high performance camshaft and a 10.25:1 compression ratio, and had polished internals, ported and gas-flowed cylinder heads, larger (1.61in/41mm diameter) inlet valves and Lucas Rita electronic ignition. Two types of carburettors were offered, initially 1⅛in Amal GP carburettors with the option of a remote float bowl, while later bikes had 32mm Amal Concentric units. These modifications gave a claimed 70bhp at 6,500rpm, a useful increase on the standard 750cc motor's claimed 60bhp, or the Combat's 65bhp. The engine retained the Isolastic mounts front and rear, but had a Norvil head steady to limit side play.

The running gear retained the standard Commando frame and had flanged alloy wheel rims, both 19in, with a WM3 width rim on the back and a WM2 width rim on the front. The front brake was a 11.5in diameter disc brake with Lockheed calliper as standard (with twin discs offered as an option), and the rear drum brake plate was ventilated. A Quaife five-speed

The first PRs featured Lockheed racing front brakes, upswept Atlas-style silencers and Fastback-type side panels.

The definitive PR was produced for 1972, with the famous bright yellow paintwork, slim Roadster-style side panels and peashooters.

The works Production Racers had a few tweaks to help increase clearance when cornering that were not available to the buying public. This example is a works JPN example in 1973 trim. The fuel tank is a TT/Endurance 5 gal.

It is possible to build your own PR, as Ken Rawlinson has done here, built up from parts and based on the 1972 and 1973 machines.

close ratio gear cluster was an option, and the exhaust system, with two separate pipes and silencers, was tucked in slightly under the engine to increase ground clearance. Upswept peashooter silencers were fitted. Clip-on handlebars and rear-set footrests completed the racing equipment. The most striking aspect of the bike was its all yellow bodywork.

A long glass fibre petrol tank (in 3½, 5 or 6 gal capacities) was complemented by a single seat with rear hump that carried the racing number plate. The rear light moulding was also in yellow,

as was the standard half fairing that carried the headlamp. Finally a slim yellow glass fibre mudguard finished off the front end.

According to Norman White, the NVPS produced 119 bikes at Thruxton between about May 1971 and June 1972. There was no special numbering system in use for the production racers and, since the bikes were based on production models, their numbers came out of the production run for the period. The bikes started around number 134872, and the final bike had the number 145182.

The Interstate tank is longer and wider than that on the Roadster, increasing the capacity to about 5 gal and the range by some 250 miles.

Commando 750 Interstate: 1972–73

The Interstate hit the market in 1972. This was Norton's take on the long-distance touring market, a role to which the Commando was very well suited owing to its vibration-free cruising, broad spread of torque and good handling. The Interstate took over this role from the Fastback LR. Its defining feature was its fuel tank, which was truly massive by the standards of the day, holding 5.2 gal (6.25 US gal/23.6ltr), but managed to appear reasonably svelte – at least in profile. The tank gave the bike a range of about 250 miles (400km) between fill ups – a significant improvement on the Roadster and Fastback and significantly better than most rivals. To help to distinguish the Interstate from the more overtly sporting Roadster (as if the huge fuel tank was not enough) and place it in its target touring market, the Interstate's side panels were large oblong units, similar to the Fastback type rather than the abbreviated triangular model seen on the Roadster. The Interstate also saw the introduction of the new Norton branded disc front brake: this was seen as a welcome improvement since the twin leading shoe brake was starting to look outmoded and the disc brake also offered a significant performance boost. The only bad news was that for 1972 the Interstate was supplied only with the Combat engine, a strange decision when out-and-out performance was not the main criteria for buying a Grand Tourer.

The Interstate featured possibly the ugliest exhaust system ever fitted to a Commando. This was a low level affair, with a kink in the exhaust pipe just before the silencer to make the silencer sit parallel to the road, just below the level of the rear wheel spindle in order that the rear wheel could be removed without disturbing the silencer. The kink destroyed the unified line of the exhaust system seen on every previous Commando and was an unfortunate styling idea that for some reason was echoed in the Hinckley Triumph T100 Bonneville of the early 2000s. The silencers were described as 'dual cone megaphones' or 'pencil cone silencers' at the time, and comprised two cones joined base

The front runners

first the sprinter...

and now a long distance strider

A bit of 1972 glamour for the introduction of the 750cc Interstate. The '72 Roadster is hiding behind the new model. An all-new disc brake was introduced in 1972 and was standard on the Interstate.

The 750 Interstate retained much of the Commando's good looks, despite the gigantic tank. Here is Les Ward's 1972 example: note the standard exhaust pipes with peashooters.

Black with gold pinstripes was a classy finish when used on the Commando: 750s had single pin stripes as standard, and 850s had twin stripes.

to base to give a fairly slim unit shaped like a stretched barrel. The thinking behind this system was actually sensible, since it allowed panniers to be fitted, but the execution was dire, with a kink in the end of the exhaust pipe to bring the pipes level that, in the author's view, ruined the lines of the bike.

The road test published in the September 1972 issue of *Motorcycle Mechanics* made the point that the offside silencer had to be removed before the rear wheel could be taken out, which was not good if there was a puncture. As an aside, the silencers do look attractive when fitted to upswept roadster exhaust pipes since they have a slim profile and are not as fat as peashooters. While the system was designed to give plenty of room for fitting luggage, Norton also missed a trick in not producing (or at least licensing) their own luggage and carrier to go with the model. While the bike was well received by the press, it was remarked that it was a bit of a cheek for the customer to buy a Grand Tourer and then have to fit his (or her) own luggage and carriers. The Interstate was the first Commando to be equipped with polished stainless steel mudguards, which were more durable than the chromed or painted ones previously fitted to the range.

The 1973 model Interstate was available with either Smiths or Italian Veglia speedo and tachometer, with the speedo having a trip function. The Veglia instruments eventually superseded the Smiths on all Commandos, but appeared on the Interstate first. The Veglia instruments were deeper than the Smiths instruments, and longer alloy pods were used, with extended bolts to fit the Smiths units. Black-painted extended lever pivots were also fitted to reduce the reach needed to use the levers.

However, the Commando's performance, lack of vibration, and its excellent handling and road holding, combined with the big fuel tank and the ability to fit luggage, made the Interstate a very competent package and an excellent basis for a long-distance tourer.

Commando 750 Racer and 750 Formula Racer: 1972

The short run of production racers seen from 1970 to 1972 was supplemented by factory-supplied kits of parts and instructions that could be used by any technically competent Commando owner to convert their road machine to PR specification.

Norton Service Release N3/12, dated August 1972, identified twelve separate kits of parts available to the customer that could be added to a standard bike to produce one to production racer or Formula 750 specification. The kits enabled a customer to build either a FIM compliant production racer, much in line with the factory-built Norvil PRs, or a 750cc Formula racer that complied with FIM regulations for Formula 750 and the USA market equivalent, as defined in the AMA (American Motorcyclist Association) rule book Chapter XIII C: & E. The service release gave detailed instructions on fitting each of the kits.

Kit 1. Engine Performance, comprising a new cylinder head with guides, new inlet and exhaust valves, valve collets, valve spring seats, a triple 'S' camshaft, new pistons and a gasket set.

Kit 2. Carburettor Accessories, comprising new inlet manifolds and washers, and new ignition switch bracket.

Kit 3. Isolastic Mounting Head Steady Assembly, comprising a new Norvil style head steady. The instructions also detail modifications to the front and rear Isolastic mounts.

Kit 4. Handlebar and Controls, Fairings, Seats, Fuel and Oil Tanks, comprising clip-on type handlebars, 3, 5 or 6 gal fuel tanks, a 750 Racer specific fairing and seat, a 750 Formula Racer specific fairing, and seat. Together with instructions on fitting the fuel tanks, seats and fairings, the Service Release has instructions on modifying the oil tank to provide clearance for the fuel tanks and seats. In addition, there are instructions on modifying the rear loop of the frame to 750 Formula specification to

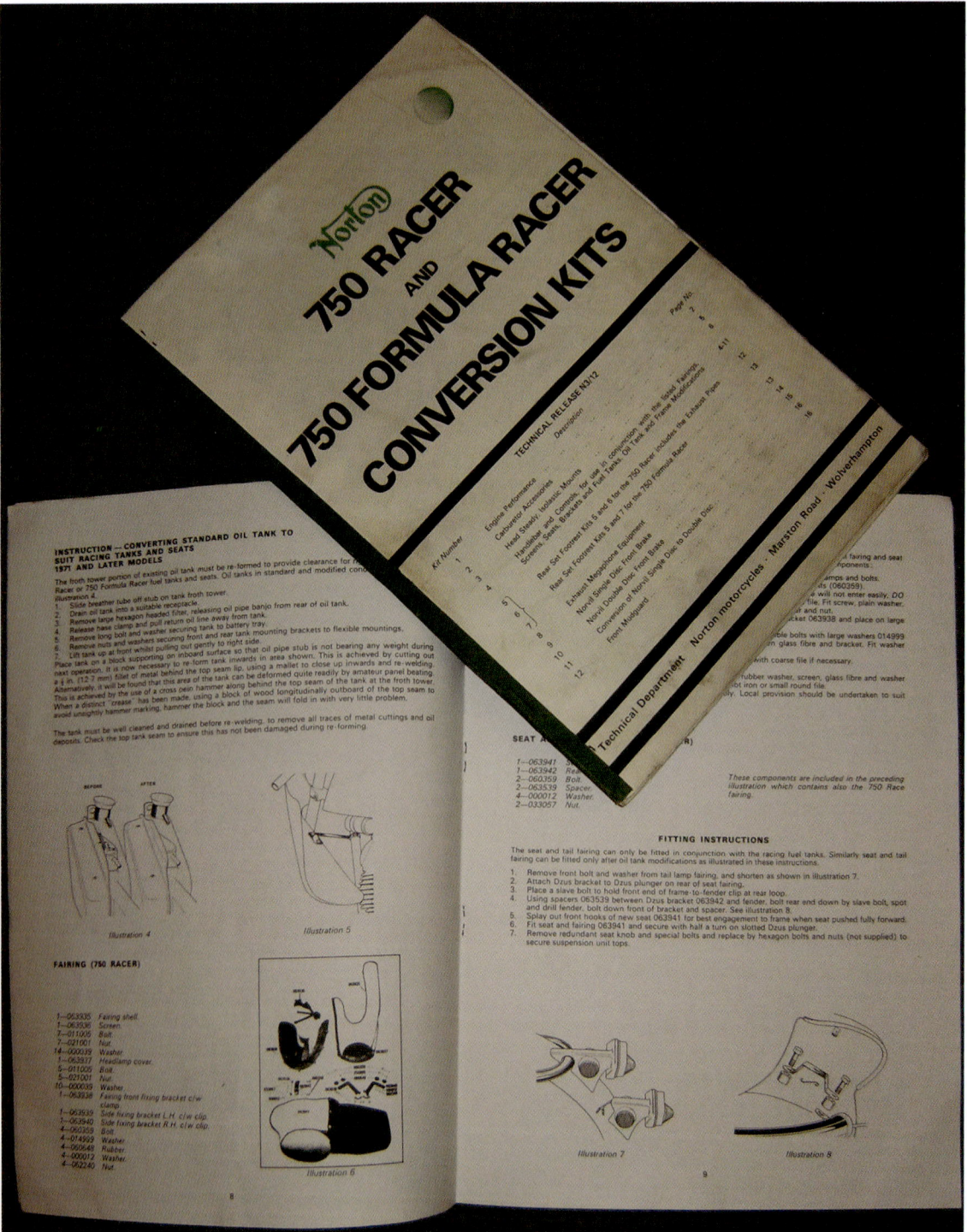

Norton produced detailed instructions on how to convert a standard bike to PR or Formula 750 specification.

The Formula 750 racer was based on production running gear and could be built by the customer using parts from the works.

accept the seat and seat fairing and give adequate tyre clearance.

Kits 5, 6 and 7. Rear set Footrests, for the 750 Racer (Kits 5 and 6) and 750 Formula Racer (Kits 5 and 7).

Kit 8. Exhaust Megaphone Equipment, specifically for the 750 Formula Racer, comprising a new racing exhaust system with racing megaphones.

Kit 9. Norvil Single Disc Front Brake, comprising a new front wheel, disc, calliper, fork slider, master cylinder and all the fittings required.

Kit 10. Norvil Double Disc Front Brake, again comprising all the components needed to fit double front discs.

Kit 11. Converting Norvil Single Disc Brake to Double Disc Assembly, comprising all components needed to convert Kit 9 to Kit 10.

The kits allowed the customer to build a racer that was compliant with the production racer and 750 Formula rules in place at the time, with parts available from the factory.

Commando 850 Roadster and Interstate Mark 1 to 2a: 1973–75

The 850 Commando was introduced in April 1973, with engine and frame numbers starting at 300,001. With a bore and stroke of 77 × 89mm, the capacity was actually 828cc, but these bikes are referred to in the text as the '850' as this was what Norton called the model and what appeared on the side panels. The new engine was designed to be a tourer rather than an out-and-out sports bike, and while the bike's running gear was similar in appearance to the 750s, it featured a large number of minor changes and continued to change as the model evolved. The 850 was introduced in the 1973 model year (retrospectively known as the Mark 1 and 1a), and was replaced with the lightly improved Mark 2 and Mark 2a for 1974. These were in turn superseded by the electric start Mark 3 in 1975.

The list of changes from the 750 made for the Mark 1 was extensive and included a number of upgrades to the running gear as well as the engine. Major changes to the engine and transmission included through bolted barrels, a 21-tooth gearbox sprocket and an exhaust balance pipe. A gauze strainer and magnetic sump plug in the crankcases helped to keep the oil clean, and an additional clutch plate and strengthened gearbox casing helped with the increased torque of the 828cc unit. The changes to the running gear included stainless steel mudguards, reinforced swing arm, revised Isolastics, hard chromed fork stanchions, a standard chrome pillion grab rail and a stiffened rear brake drum. All 850s featured double pinstripes on the tank and side panels, offering a quick recognition aid for the spotter. The Mark 1 was marketed in Roadster, Interstate, Interpol and Hi-Rider versions. Its running gear was virtually the same as the current 750.

The new 850 Mk1 Roadster and Interstate looked similar to the 750 models but were in different colours and had 850 badges.

The 850 Mark 1a was the first Commando to wear the 'bean can' silencers and also had a new black plastic air box. Both of these changes were to cut down the noise levels for the European market.

The larger engine was the main difference, distinguished from the 750 by its new cylinder casting to accommodate the through bolts fixing the head and barrel to the crankcases. The Mark 1 retained the 32mm Amal Concentric carburettors seen on the 750, and these units (L932/29 on the right and L932/30 on the left) now came with drain plugs in the float bowl and 'Spanish' ticklers, which featured a shroud over the tickler that made them easier to use and prevented rainwater draining into the float bowl. In addition the exhaust pipes were joined by a balance pipe close to the exhaust ports. The Mark 1 Interstate retained the low, non-upswept exhaust pipes and long taper silencers from the 750 models, while the Roadster and Hi-Rider both had upswept pipes with peashooters.

In the early 1970s various European countries, particularly Germany, were introducing stringent noise regulations for motorcycles. While the Mark 1 850 was already quieter than the 750, thanks to the exhaust balance pipe, more work would be needed to meet Germany's new standard of a maximum of 84dB. This led to the introduction of the Mark 1a variant of the 850 in October 1973. The Roadster and Interstate bikes sported large 'black cap' peripheral discharge silencers and a new air box and cleaner assembly. These silencers were designed in conjunction with Manchester University and comprised three concentric cylinders. The exhaust gases were directed through the centre cylinder, which ran the length of the silencer, and were then diffused through holes in the periphery of the tube into the second cham-

This 850 Roadster sports a single Mikuni carburettor – a popular conversion – and has a non-standard air cleaner.

ber, where they ran 'backwards' through a series of baffles into the third chamber, reversing direction again so they exited in the gap between the black cap and the outer skin of the silencer. The result was a very efficient silencer that was very quiet and, contrary to popular belief, caused virtually no performance penalty: the perceived drop in performance of the 850 over the 750 was down to the air box. The air box was a large plastic moulding and was longer than the previous air cleaner assembly, and took up some of the space usually taken by the battery on the previous 750 and 850 Mark 1. Air was sucked into the box via two intake 'ears' at the bottom of the air box, which could be removed fairly easily to push the power (and noise levels) up. An oiled foam air cleaner was fitted in the air box. The battery carrier was redesigned and the battery was turned through 90 degrees and sited further back, mounted transversely behind the air box between the oil tank and the side panel. In addition to these obvious external modifications, the model received alterations to the gearing: a higher second gear ratio

and a 22-tooth gearbox sprocket to lower the revs when being subjected to the formal test, which included runs past the noise meter in second gear.

The 850 Mark 2 was introduced in late 1973 for the 1974 season, and was mainly sold in the USA as the Roadster, Interstate and Hi-Rider. This model sported black barrels, peashooter silencers for the Roadster and Hi-Rider and low-level dual cone silencers for the Interstate. The model had the Mark 1 type paper air filter behind its perforated metal cover, as the US noise regulations were not as stringent as those being implemented in the European markets. The 850 Mark 2 also featured rubber lower covers on the black-finished longer instrument pods. The 32mm Amal Concentric carburettors remained, but the ports were modified to taper down to 30mm as on the earlier 750s. This improved the power and eliminated a flat spot between 3,000 and 4,000rpm suffered by the Mark 1 850. The Mark 2 850 also sported a black-painted cylinder barrel, and featured a number of further improvements including a black plastic grease catcher on the end of the chain guard, which prevented chain lube from coating the rear of the bike, a halogen headlight and a longer kick start lever.

The Mark 2a was introduced at the same time as the Mark 2 in late 1973 and was aimed at UK and Europe market with its more restrictive noise legislation. It retained the Mark 1a's silencing efforts with the 'black cap' peripheral discharge silencers for the Roadster, Interstate and Hi-Rider and the new, larger air box in black plastic, with its intake ears on the bottom. The Mark 2a was a well sorted machine that was quick, handled well and was reliable. It remained in production until the introduction of the electric start Mark 3 in 1975 with only a few minor modifications, comprising a new quick action twist grip, a metering clip for the rear chain oiler, a new pair of second gears in the gearbox, a revised rear chainguard extension and a new battery holding bar. To many people the 850cc Mark 2a Commando represents the pinnacle of the Commando as a fast, sport-oriented and touring bike. The Mark 3 that followed it, while being more sophisticated and refined was softer and not aimed at a high performance.

An 850 Mark 1 or Mark 2 Roadster, retaining the standard 750 style air filter.

This 850 Roadster has an uprated front disc brake, with modified mudguard stay.

The standard Mark 2a was a handsome beast, as this Candy Apple Red Interstate (above left) and JPN Blue Stripe Roadster (above right) demonstrate. Note that the Blue Stripe does not have a red pinstripe, as the Mark 3 was to feature.

The short stoke 750 was very similar in appearance to the 850, although without the pinstripes.

Commando Short Stroke 750 Roadster: 1973

With the introduction of the 850 range in April 1973, Norton did not abandon the 750 market completely, especially as this was a popular racing capacity in both production racing and the Formula 750. As described in Chapter 4, Technical Description and Development Norton produced a 750cc motor based on the new 850 unit, which shared the new bore of 77mm but had a reduced stroke of 80mm, in contrast to the original 750's bore and stroke of 73 × 89mm. This engine unit was sold separately, but Norton produced a number of complete bikes (some sources say fewer than 200). These bikes were produced either in John Player Norton Café Racer or standard Roadster trim. The Roadsters were coloured red in the brochure and did not have pinstripes on the steel tank and side panels. They carried 750 Commando transfers on the side panels and were fully equipped for road use, including full lights and indicators. The exhaust system did not have the 850's balance pipe. A tuning kit of 33mm carburettors, bell mouths and megaphone exhausts was also available, which boosted power up to a claimed 80bhp at the crank at 8,000rpm.

The John Player Norton was named after the sponsors of the works racers. It was a Café Racer variant of the Mark 2a.

John Player Norton: 1974–75

The John Player Norton (also sometimes called the John Player Special) was Norton's final niche market special and was a fully road-legal café racer. It was probably the first such production offering from a British factory since Royal Enfield produced their 250cc Crusader Sports and Continental models in the mid-1960s. The bike was based on the Mark 2a 850 with its new quieter air box and was offered with either the 828cc engine in standard tune or with the short stroke 750cc unit as 'a base for competition' – and to use up the remaining 750cc short stroke engines that Norton had to produce to homologate them for production racing. The John Player Norton had a total production run of around 200: it is not clear how many of the 750cc versions were produced, but the majority were 850s.

The bike was styled by NVT designer Mike Ofield and looked the business, with a John Player Norton racer inspired three-quarter racing-style fairing, tank cover and seat unit, which was complete with the high level aerodynamic seat hump. In essence, however, the bike (in 850cc guise) was simply a reclothed Mark 2a. The glass fibre tank cover was fixed over a 3 gal (3.5 US gal/13.6ltr) steel fuel tank, unique to the model, and was also attached to the inside edge of the fairing along its base, mimicking the appearance of the F750 pannier tanks.

The fairing closely followed the styling of the F750 unit with aerodynamic bulges on each side to shield the rider's hands, and extended down to the top of the crankcases to protect the rider's upper legs. The indicators were mounted on the lower front sides of the fairing, and the lower front side also had the obligatory amber reflector.

Red and blue styling flashes cut from vinyl were placed on the fairing sides and on the sides of the seat hump, which also carried a Union flag between the flashes. The early 850 Mark 2

Black chrome exhausts and silencers helped promote the Café Racer theme.

brochure shows the fairing flashes as three horizontal lines, red top, then white then blue, but the production variant, shown in the later 850 Mark 2 brochure, had a tapered pattern that started as a pair of thin red and blue lines just behind each headlamp, which widened as the line flowed back, turning downwards to match the line of the rear edge of the fairing, and ending as two broad bands. The fairing flashes also had the words 'John Player Norton' on the bottom of the flash. The red and blue were separated by a thin white divider.

The speedometer, tachometer and standard three warning lights were installed on a black dash panel under the windscreen. A slim glass fibre front mudguard and black chrome exhaust system with balance pipe and peripheral discharge silencers continued the sporting look, and clip-on handlebars and rear-set footrests finished off the racy appearance. A neat touch was the choke lever mounted on a short chromed bar clamped to the top yoke using the standard handlebar clamps. The brochure promised a personalized name decal for any purchaser, which would appear just below the fairing's screen. The fairing carried twin 5¾in diameter 45/40 watt headlamps, and the electrical system was beefed up with a high output alternator and twin Zener diodes to handle the extra load. As the model was based on the Mark 2a, the bike retained the restrictive Mark 2a plastic air box and the 2a battery carrier, where the battery is mounted further back and across the bike to make room for the larger air box.

The John Player Norton was only produced alongside the Mark 2a 850 models for 1974 and 1975. The UK and US brochures for the Mark 3 both show a JPN model, and the pictures clearly show it has a left foot gear change, rear disc and the front disc mounted ahead of the drive side fork slider, so at least one Mark 3 JPN was built. However, the model does not appear to have been formally put into production as a Mark 3.

The fairing sides were integrated with the tank cover to form a rigid and attractive windcheater.

Clip-on handlebars and standard speedo, tacho and warning lights mounted on the fairing dash panel gave the pilot a racing-style experience.

The Thruxton Club racer was produced in 1975 and was based on a prototype produced by Norman White.

Commando 750 Thruxton Club Racer: 1975

The Club Racer was a small production run of some thirty machines produced by the race department at Thruxton to cater for the private short circuit racers of the day. The bikes were not road legal and were produced to help to finance the race department, and used the remaining 750cc short stroke motors originally produced to homologate the 1973 850cc-based 750cc motor for F750 racing. The bike was closely based on the PR machine and was developed by Norman White from a successful racer originally built and raced by him in 1974. The bikes featured a nickel-plated frame and were marketed to the club racers exclusively by Gus Kuhn, the London-based Norton dealer. Notable changes from the Production Racer were the use of a rear disc brake with Lockheed calliper, a Quaife five-speed gearbox as standard, and clutch outrigger bearing was used. The bodywork was in glass fibre and the design, while unique to the bike, was based loosely on the F750 John Player Norton and so shared the hand protection, but had a neatly integrated seat and tank unit with flowing lines.

The bike was not particularly successful, due to opposition from the likes of the easily available and relatively cheap lightweight Yamaha TZ350 two-stroke, and it really served to show that the days of the big four-stroke racers were over.

Commando 850 Roadster, Interstate, Hi-Rider and Interpol Mark 3: 1975–77

The final Commando model was the 829cc Mark 3, which was introduced in February 1975. The bike was introduced by Norton Villiers Triumph alongside the Triumph T160 Trident and was described as the tourer of the pair, with the Trident being marketed as the sports machine. The defining feature of the model was the electric start, which finally bought the Commando into line with the Japanese competition.

The Thruxton Club's bodywork was unique, but was based on the F750. A standard Smiths mechanical rev counter was fitted.

The Mark 3's defining feature was the electric start, mounted on the back of the primary chain case. The left-foot gear change was fitted to meet US legislation.

As well as the new starter, there were a large number of changes and improvements designed to enable the Commando to compete in the home and overseas markets. The result was a machine that was greatly refined and more easy to live with than the Mark 2, but which was softer, heavier and not so sporting. To satisfy the US market's legal demands, the gear change was moved to the left-hand side and the gearbox action was reversed to give a one down, three up shift pattern to match other manufacturers' machines on the market. The crossover linkage used to provide the left-foot change meant that the gearbox had to be fixed in position so an automatic hydraulic chain tensioner was fitted to keep the primary chain tension correct.

The switch to left-foot gear changing also led to the adoption of a rear disk brake: the unit was identical to the front and it was probably easier to engineer the hydraulically operated mechanism than it was to engineer a crossover mechanism to operate the original rear drum, and of course a rear disc was quite novel and a good selling point at the time. A simple recognition point for the Mark 3 was the front disc calliper, which was moved to the front of the left-hand fork leg. This was supposed to remove the tendency for the earlier disc-braked bikes to pull to the left. The Isolastic mountings also gained the 'vernier' adjustment method specified in the original patent, making it possible to adjust the clearances of the Isolastics by screwing in the outer plates, removing the need to use shims. A new spring located head steady was also specified, which kept the two rubber mounts but added a pair of springs at the front, which helped to centralize the engine weight across the two lower Isolastic mounts, improving their ability to absorb the engine vibration. The electrics were beefed up, with a larger battery to power the starter, a 180 watt high

The Mark 3 Interstate made an excellent tourer. The large tank and long gearing made it a capable mile-eater.

The new rear disc brake needed a new right-hand side pedal to operate it.
Standard 'bean can' or black cap silencers are fitted to this example.

output alternator and dual Zener diode charging system, as previously seen on the Mark 2a John Player Norton, new ergonomically designed black-painted and modern-looking handlebar switchgear with forged alloy levers, and a small idiot light and ignition switch console positioned between the speedometer and tachometer. A new seat, hinged on its left-hand side and lockable (at last), gave easy access to the oil filler cap. Strengthened crankcases, revised oil system and screws around the periphery of the chain case helped to keep the oil inside the engine.

The headline change, and the one most eagerly awaited by the press and punters, was the electric start. The system was a bit marginal: it was described as electric assistance by some testers, and even the rider's handbook says 'for the first start of the day and particularly during very cold weather' the starter could be 'supplemented by the kick starter'. The official way to start the engine, as documented in the rider's handbook, was to use short 'jabs' on the starter button. This technique was intended to push the motor over compression and the heavy flywheel would then carry the crank over the next compression stroke and the engine would fire. If it did not, then the drill was to try again – but the manual advises not to just hold the button down as that would swiftly flatten the battery. The handbook also tells the user not to have the lights on when trying to start. The American-made Prestolite ('Press to Light') starter motor, while more powerful than the Lucas M3 unit fitted to the contemporary Triumph T160 Trident and Norton's earlier foray into electric starting with the 1963 400cc Electra, was only just man enough for the job. It can be modified with extra brushes to increase its power, and thicker wires from the solenoid to the motor also help as the standard ones were marginal.

Despite these quirks, the electric starter could work reasonably well and was pretty good when the battery was fully charged and the engine was warm. The rest of the modifications made to the Mark 3 gave an excellent machine, well suited to the touring role of the Interstate and the fast road use of the Roadster. Norton advertised the electric start's presence with 'Electric Start' written under the 850 Commando decal on the side panel of the Mark 3. The bikes were well received by the press and received mainly favourable reports. The Trident was viewed as the sportster in the range, with the Commando being a softer, more relaxed tourer, with a claimed weight of 430lb (195kg) blunting the performance, which had also been progressively reduced by increased restrictions on inlet and exhaust noise. By now the range had been reduced to the Interstate, Roadster and Interpol in the UK and the Interstate, Roadster and a few Hi-Riders for the USA. Colours were Black or Candy Apple Red, with White with Blue stripe scheme exclusively for the Roadster and Manx Silver with black and red lining for the Interstate. The Interpol came in white as usual.

The Mark 3 remained in production on and off until late 1977, when the last production batch of some 1,400 models trickled out of the Wolverhampton works supervised by the official receiver. Some of these were still available new at dealers in the UK into 1978. The October 1977 issue of Bike magazine tested one of the Interstates from this last batch and put it into a Giant test with a Honda CB750K7 and it came out pretty much equal to the Honda, with both bikes being seen as touring rather than sporting mounts. Probably the most telling comment was that the tester found the relative crudity of the Norton to be a refreshing change from the sani-tized Japanese fours he was used to. When the final batch of Mark 3s rolled out of the Wolverhampton factory, that was it for the mass production of the Commando.

Commando Performance

When it was introduced in 1968 the Commando was right at the top of the performance tree. With 750cc, giving around 60bhp and a relatively light weight, the bike sported lightning acceleration and a high top speed. Early road tests demonstrated this with some very impressive performance figures returned. The accompanying tables reproduce road test data from various bike magazines (*Motor Cycle Mechanics* and *Bike* from the UK and *Cycle World* and *Cycle Guide* from the US).

Interestingly the performance figures obtained by the UK magazine were better than those posted by the US tests, perhaps reflecting a partisan attitude by the magazines or the factory supplying specially prepared bikes for test in the UK. The difference in top-end performance between the 750cc and 850cc models is quite marked: the figures show how the top speed dropped slightly as the design aged, but the acceleration figures remained remarkably consistent through to the introduction of the Mark 3 in 1975. At this point the acceleration over the quarter mile has gone down significantly, but the 0–60 and top speed figures are pretty close to the Mark 2a, which tends to go against the public perception that the Mark 3's performance was significantly less than that of the earlier models. Overall the Commando's performance reflected its role as it evolved from being a top of the range road burner into a very capable long-distance tourer.

Rescue Mission: The Norton 76

As Norton slipped into liquidation, a group of workers from the Norton factory in Wolverhampton formed a group called the Wolverhampton Action Committee (WAC). At the same time the British Norton Partnership, a consortium formed by Australian businessman Ronald Titcombe and Lord Hesketh, was trying to put the finance together to save Norton. The plan was to do a quick update of the Commando to give the factory breathing space, and a product to sell, until new models such as the stepped piston 500cc Wulf could enter production. The Norton 76 was the updated Commando. It was produced in early 1976 and shown to the UK press before it was shipped out to the USA for display at the Daytona bike week, where it received a good reaction. Finance was not forthcoming, however, the British Norton Partnership was dissolved and the Norton 76 became one of many 'might have beens' as the British motorcycle industry slowly died.

So was the Norton 76 just a gently warmed-over Commando or something more? Essentially it took the good bits and added better suspension, better fuel consumption and better brakes. According to the only contemporary road test, published in *Bike* magazine in April 1977, the bike was better than the factory offering.

The WAC went to Italy for new suspension and running gear, with Paioli front forks, FPS cast alloy wheels, and Brembo disc brakes: two at the front and one at the rear.

The front master cylinder was mounted remotely and cable operated from the handlebars. On the test, however, only one disc was connected, so braking was not as good as it should have been. The cylinder head was modified to remove the squish band, providing a full hemispherical shape. This was done primarily to clean up emissions. Probably the most significant modification was the replacement of the standard pair of 32mm Amal Concentrics with a single 1½in (40mm) SU constant velocity carburettor. This not only improved the emissions, but cut fuel consumption by a claimed 40 per cent.

The main cosmetic change was the fuel tank, which was a standard roadster tank modified with filler to give the intended shape of a modern-looking 4 gal unit. Thanks to the better fuel economy of the SU carburettor, this would give the Norton 76 the same range as the Interstate, but without the width of the larger tank. There was also a modified instrument panel with brake pad wear and hydraulic fluid warning lights, in addition to the Mark 3's high beam, indicator, charge and neutral.

LEFT: *The Norton 76 was an updated Commando produced to try and save the Commando during 1976.*
CENTRE: *The Norton 76 sported an SU carburettor and a restyled fuel tank.*
RIGHT: *Unmistakably a Commando, but Paioli front forks and Brembo brakes were used, as British equivalents were no longer available.*

The Mark 3 Roadster still looked slim and sporty. Here it is in JPN colours.

The twin uprated front brakes on this 850 Mark 3 show what can be done to upgrade the machine.

UK Market Test Results

	750 Fastback	750 Commando 'S'	750 Interstate Combat	850 Mark 1 Roadster	850 Mk2a Roadster	1975 850 Mk 3 Interstate
Source	*Motor Cycle Mechanics*	*Motor Cycle Mechanics*	*Motor Cycle Mechanics*	*Motor Cycle Mechanics*	*Motor Cycle Mechanics*	*Bike*
Date of test	August 1968	December 1969	September 1972	June 1973	Jan '74	May 1975
Power (bhp)	58	58	65	60	58	58
Top speed (mph / km/h)	121 / 195	124 / 200	122 / 196	120 / 193	110 / 177	111 / 179
0–60 (secs)	5	5.2	4.5	4.9	6.0	5.5
Standing start ¼ mile (secs)	12.8	13.4	12.2	12.9	12.5	14.24

US Market Test Results

	750 Fastback	750 Fastback	750 Roadster	Mark 1 850 Interstate	850 Mk 3 Interstate (N.B. with fairing)
Source	*Cycle World*	*Cycle World*	*Cycle Guide*	*Cycle World*	*Cycle World*
Date of test	September 1968	March 1971	September 1972	May 1972	Dec 75
Power (bhp)	N/A	60	65	60	N/A
Top speed (mph / km/h)	114.5 / 184	116.4 / 187	109.5 / 176	116 / 187	94 / 151
0–60 (secs)	5.5	5.4	7.0	5.0	6.0
Standing start ¼ mile (secs)	13.47	13.11	13.09	12.96	14.9

Norton Commando 961

In 2005 Norton Motorsports Inc., a US-based company run by long-term Norton Commando enthusiast Kenny Dreer, unveiled a new Commando. This was not a rehash of the old Commando but a new interpretation of the model, sporting a brand new 961cc vertical twin, with pushrod operated valve in an all new frame designed by C & J Racing Frames, who had made the frames for the Ron Wood Norton flat trackers in the late 1970s (see Chapter 4). The engine was designed to look like the Commando unit with forward tilted barrels; the timing side even featured an interpretation of the Commando timing cover with the Norton script cast in. The frame was built from 4130 Chrome-moly tubing and the front forks were state-of-the-art 43mm diameter Olins units. The rear suspension used twin Olins shock absorbers again and the wheels were 17in diameter cast six-spoke forged alloy units. The bike was tested by a number of press riders and well received, but it never made it into production.

Fast forward to 2010, when Norton Motorcycles (UK) Ltd, based at Donington Park Grand Prix Circuit, is producing and delivering new Commando 961s. A UK entrepreneur, Stuart Garner, has spent much time and money buying the Norton name and the rights to the Kenny Dreer prototypes, and preparing to manufacture the bikes. While the UK bikes look very similar to the Dreer prototypes, they are completely re-engineered and share very few components with the 2005 bike.

The re-engineered engine is a parallel twin with two valve heads and a 270-degree crank with single balance shaft to protect against the twin cylinder vibes. The overhead valves are, in true Commando tradition, operated by push rods but feature hydraulic operation to avoid noise. The engine produces a claimed 80bhp at 6,500rpm and an impressive 90Nm of torque at 5,200rpm. The air- and oil-cooled engine has extensive finning of the alloy head and cylinder barrels, and sports a small oil cooler mounted on down tubes. It is a dry sump design, with the oil carried in the frame. The bike also features fuel injection and a three-way catalytic converter to meet the modern Euro 3 emissions standards. A gear-driven primary drive and a five-speed gearbox in unit with the engine completed the picture. The frame is an all tubular unit again closely based on the Dreer/C & J unit and is of all tubular construction. The rear swinging arm is rectangular in cross-section and the suspension front and rear is by Swedish manufacturer Ohlins. The twin front and single rear disc brakes are by Brembo. The new Commando was introduced to the market early in 2010 as a limited edition model, the high specification 961SE. This model was distinguished by the use of carbon fibre for the wheels, front mudguard, headlamp mounts, rear hugger, chain guard and rear number plate hanger. The limited number of these bikes sold out quickly and two new models were introduced, the Café Racer and the Sport. The Café Racer is the sports version, with clip-on handlebars and has 43mm Ohlins upside-down forks with Brembo Gold Line radial-mounted front brake callipers and spoked wheels, and is finished off with a small solid front wind deflector in front of the instruments. The Sport, the lower priced model, is a bit more conservative with 'normal' handlebars, conventional 43mm Ohlins forks and axially mounted front brake callipers, while sharing the spoked wheels.

One aspect of the Dreer bikes that Garner kept was the styling. This is probably best described as being a modern take on the generic Commando looks, with the engine retaining the look of the Commando, the tank and side panels being loosely styled on the original Commando Roadster unit (but holding a useful 4 gal (17ltr). The silencers on the SE and Sports are dead ringers for the famous Norton peashooters. This semi-retro styling is reinforced with a range of traditional Norton colours. Colour schemes include black with gold pinstripes, Manx (and Commando Mark 3) style silver with black and red pinstriping, Candy Red with silver pinstripes and the traditional PR Yellow. The fuel tanks sport traditional Norton script decals and the original 'Commando', albeit subtly updated, appears on the side panels along with the '961' capacity. Press reception has been universally good and the bikes look to be worthy successors to the Commando name.

Norton Motorcycles (UK) Ltd can be contacted at Donington Park Grand Prix Circuit, Donington Park, Castle Donington, Derby DE74 2RP (Tel.: 01332 811988, www.nortonmotorcycles.com).

All three: the full line-up of the new Commandos, (from left to right) 961SE, Café Racer and Sport.

The Café Racer has clip-on handlebars and sports upside-down Ohlins forks.

The first new Commando, the limited edition 961 SE, features extensive carbon fibre parts and top specification running gear.

The Sport is the current model, seen here in red. Its lower specification running gear is reflected in its lower price.

3 Technical Description and Development

After its introduction in 1968, the Commando was continuously developed. The most significant stages in its development were probably the introduction of the Combat engine in 1972 and the 850 engine in 1973, and the final electric start Mark 3 version in 1975. From year to year, as new models and different paint schemes were added to the range, the bikes were also improved and refined mechanically.

The sections in this chapter look at the overall design of the Commando and the changes that were made throughout the life of the bike.

Engine Layout and Design

The 750cc Commando engine was typical of the twins being produced by the British industry, and had a venerable ancestry even when introduced, with its obvious derivation from Bert Hopwood's 500cc Dominator engine of the late 1940s. The first Commando engines were very obviously lightly modified Atlas units that had been around since the early 1960s: the external clues were the ignition points placed in the old magneto position behind the rear top corner of the timing cover, and the tachometer drive taken from the end of the camshaft with the drive mounted on the outside of the timing cover. Early Commando timing covers did not have the 'Norton' name in traditional script cast into the face of the timing cover, a feature that first appeared in mid-1969.

The engine was a parallel twin (that is, with the cylinders in a side-by-side configuration) with a 360 degree crank. This meant that the crank pins were on the same axis, and the pistons went up and down together and fired on alternate cycles (when one piston was on its firing stroke the other was on its exhaust stroke). This configuration gave smooth power pulses, but poor primary balance, and this gave rise to vibration. When the 750cc Norton motor was used in the Featherbed-framed Atlas the vibration was generally considered to be approaching the unacceptable, hence the need for the Isolastic system to protect the rider from the parallel twin vibes.

While Norton did not follow Triumph and BSA's lead in adopting unit construction for the Commando's power plant, the bike's engine followed conventional British design themes with light alloy crankcases, cast iron barrels and an

Early Commandos had their contact breaker points positioned in the old magneto position behind the rear of the timing cover.

alloy one-piece cylinder head. Again in common with the British competition it featured pushrod-operated overhead valves, two valves per cylinder, an alternator driven from the left-hand side of the crank and ancillaries (oil pump, ignition contact breakers and camshaft) driven from the timing side.

Unlike the BSA and Triumph unit twins, Norton drove the forward-mounted camshaft and initially the ignition points (while they were in the old magneto position) with short chains. The camshaft was driven from the outer ring of a double sprocket mounted outboard of the half-speed idler gear driven off the crank pinion. The argument for keeping it was less noise, but it was also probably cheaper to do it that way. On the first Commando engines, the ignition contact breaker points and centrifugal advance retard unit were housed in a neat alloy casing in the position occupied by the magneto on earlier versions of the unit at the top rear of the timing cover. The

unit was driven by a second chain driven from the inner sprocket on the half-speed idler pinion. Also nestling in the timing cover was the gear type oil pump. The pump was driven by a worm gear on the end of the crankshaft and had two chambers: one to pump oil into the engine and one to scavenge the oil back from the sump to the oil tank.

The lubrication system followed standard British bike practice for the time. Drillings in the crankcases and timing case fed the oil from the feed side of the pump, via a pressure relief valve, to the end of the crankshaft, where further drillings in the crankshaft led it to the big ends. Once the oil passed through the big ends it sprayed out into the crankcases to lubricate the barrels, pistons, main bearings and small ends and it also helped to cool the pistons. The oil then fell down into the bottom of the crankcases where it was scavenged back to the oil tank. Further drillings from the pressure side fed oil via an

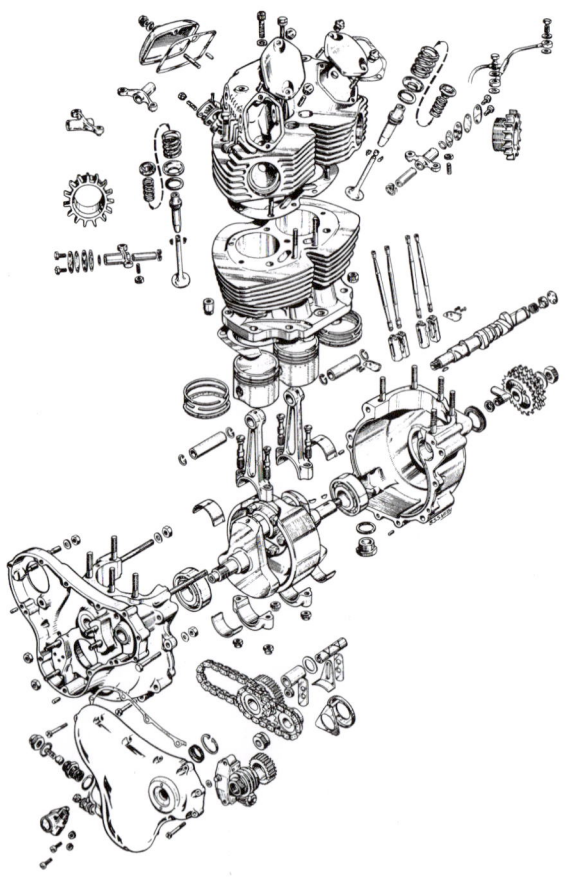

The engine followed 'standard' British practice: two cylinders, side by side with parallel crank pins, so that the pistons rise up and down together, giving a firing stroke on each revolution.

The lubrication system was again standard British fare. Later bikes had a full-flow oil filter plumbed into the oil return line, an easy retro fit.

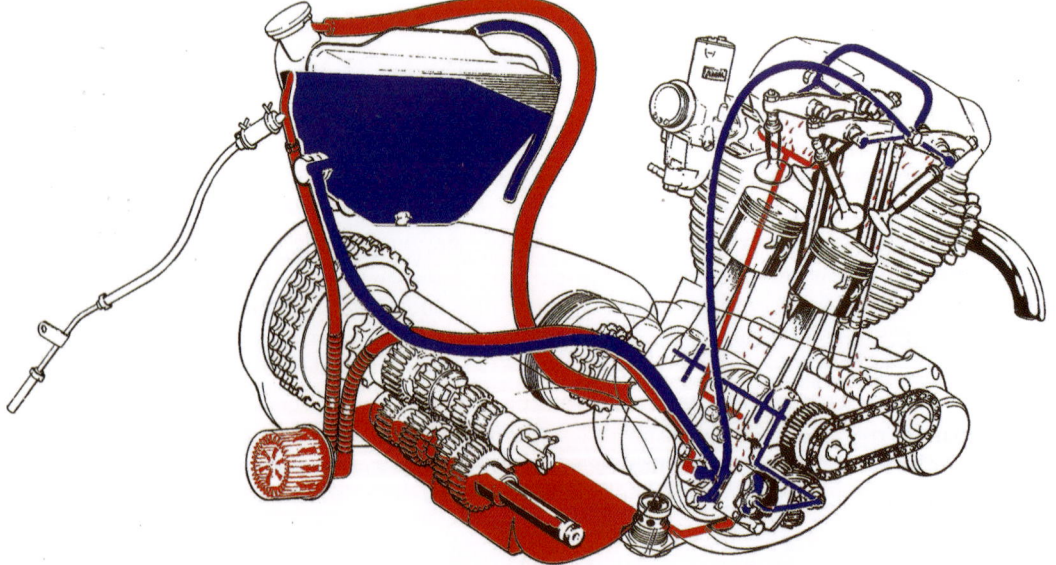

external pipe up to the cylinder head to lube the valves and rockers. This oil then drained down the pushrod tunnel, lubricating the cam followers and camshaft on its way down to the sump. Initially oil filtration was crude: a gauze filter in the oil tank feed prevented large particles from getting into the pressure side. Up to and including the 1971 models a second gauze filter was placed in the sump to protect the scavenge side. This was deleted on the 1972 models but reintroduced for the 1973 750 and 850 models.

The cast iron barrels were bolted to the crankcases by nine studs and nuts and had a cast-in pushrod tunnel over the cam at the front of the engine. There were air passages each side of the tunnel to allow cooling air to pass between the bores, and the whole casting was extensively finned. The cam followers were fitted directly into the base of the barrel and were lubricated by excess oil from the head making its way down the pushrod tunnel.

The head on the 750 engine was held on to the barrels by nine fixings, a combination of bolts and studs. The four outer fixings (two each side) were bolts, as was one central front fixing. There were three studs in the head, two at the front and one at the back, and these were fixed in place with nuts that were carefully hidden among the barrels' fins. The front two nuts were long to aid access. Finally there were two studs at the front of the barrel, in front of the push rod tunnel, that mated with nuts in tunnels at the front of the head. The head itself was a single alloy casting, with parallel inlet ports and widely splayed exhaust ports to ensure good cooling; this was a fundamental consideration that Bert Hopwood designed into the original 500cc unit after seeing the cooling problems experienced by Edward Turner on his iron headed Speed Twin unit. This valve configuration required the use of four separate rocker shafts to carry each valve's operating gear. The rocker shafts were carried in the head casting itself, rather than following Triumph's leak-prone separate rocker box approach, and were pressed into blind drillings in the head. The spindles were held in place by distinctive small lozenge-shaped covers, which also sealed in the oil. Oil was fed from the pressure side of the oil

The barrels on the 750 are bolted to the crankcases using nine studs and nuts.

The 750 cylinder head is cast alloy with widely spaced exhaust ports for good cooling. Ten bolts and studs hold it firmly on the barrels.

The later 750 had the tacho drive repositioned in front of the barrels and the contact breaker points placed in the front top of the timing cover.

pump via a flexible pipe from the rear of the timing side to a single point on each side of the head, where drillings led to each inlet and exhaust spindle. Access to the valve gear for adjustment was good, with a single alloy cover on the inlets and a domed alloy cover over each exhaust.

The engine breathing system was a typical British solution of the time, a timed breather valve driven off the end of the camshaft, which exited from the front drive side of the engine via an elbow and pipe that travelled back along the cases just below the barrels and vented into the oil tank.

The first developments to the engine were introduced in 1969 and were initially seen on the 'S' model and on the Commando Fastback and 'R' (after engine number 131257). The points were moved from their housing in the old magneto position and were rehoused on the end of the camshaft. This meant a new timing cover with a cast alloy points cover at the front, and Norton took the opportunity to cast the 'Norton' name

into the cover at the same time. The camshaft was modified to carry the then industry standard Lucas advance and retard unit on a taper, and the new timing case had an oil seal that ran on the end of the camshaft to keep oil out of the points. The twin contact breaker points were Lucas 6CA type, individually mounted on a plate that screwed to the new timing cover. These points allowed separate adjustment for each set, giving very fine control over ignition timing. As the points took the place originally occupied by the tachometer drive, this was moved to the front top of the timing side crankcase, where it was held on by two screws and was driven by a skew gear on the camshaft. This drive would be a source of slight oil leakage until the end of production.

The chain that used to drive the points in the magneto position was deleted and the drive pinion was also revised to carry just one sprocket to drive the camshaft. The old contact breaker points position on the rear of the timing chest was covered with a steel plate.

The 750 engine continued with minor changes until the end of 1971. Big changes were then introduced at the start of 1972. Norton ditched the consecutive numbering system at the same time, starting the 1972 models from 200,000. At this point the motor received new crankcases, with reinforced main bearing webs and walls that were generally thicker all round. The main bearings were strengthened, with a roller bearing fitted on the timing side. Strangely the scavenge side filter was deleted from the new cases, and the repositioned scavenge pickup led to problems with oil return at sustained high revs. The lubrication system benefited from a full flow oil filter fitted in the return feed from the engine, which was presumably the justification for deleting the sump filter. The scavenge pickup could be badly affected by oil aeration, especially when run hard and fast, resulting in lowered oil pressure. The engine breather was changed completely. The camshaft driven timed valve was removed and a breather casing was bolted to the rear of the crankcases. This was fed from the cases and contained a gauze separator to retain oil mist, and a large diameter pipe that led directly

Les Ward's 1972 Interstate engine appears to have never been apart, and would have been to Combat specification. The Combat engines came with black-painted barrels.

upwards and was vented into the oil tank. This newly strengthened, but still flawed engine formed the basis for Norton's most famous (or infamous) engine variant: the Combat.

With eyes firmly on the competition, Norton wanted to up the power given by the Commando to compete with the new 750cc superbikes, such as the Honda CB750, the Triumph Trident and the Kawasaki 750 triple. The tune-up was achieved quite simply: a hot SS camshaft was mated with larger 32mm diameter carburettors on enlarged and gas flowed ports. The compression ratio was raised from 9:1 to 10:1 by skimming the head, while using the same pistons as the standard engine. The Combat head was designated RH3 by the factory and was supposed to have had a 'C' stamped on the top. The engine power was increased to a claimed 65bhp at 6,500rpm, against a standard claimed 60bhp at 6,800rpm. The Combat specification engine was (somewhat bizarrely) introduced as a standard fitment on the new Interstate models and as an option for the Roadster and Fastback, and the barrels were painted black. The first Combat

engine was numbered 200976. The woes of the Combat Commando centred on an unhappy crankshaft and crankcase relationship. While the beefed-up cases could cope with the additional power and were very stiff, the bolt up crank was just too flexible, and would whip, especially when revved above 7,000rpm. Short gearing with a standard 19-tooth gearbox sprocket and a willing, free-breathing engine encouraged the rider to rev the engine and, with no vibration to discourage them, this meant over-revving was the order of the day. The flexing crankshaft caused the edges of the rollers in the main bearings to dig into their bearing housings, resulting in rapid wear, lots of metallic particles floating round the cases, and grumbling mains often after as few as 4,000 miles.

To give Norton their due, they quickly recognized the problem and instigated a programme to sort it out. The factory identified the bearing issue and fitted the now famous 'Superblends', which had barrel-shaped rollers that could accommodate the crankshaft whip. Superblends were fitted as standard from July and it is pretty unlikely that there are any running Commando engines that have not had them retrofitted by now. Norton retrofitted Superblends to all the bikes they had in stock and also took steps to lower the compression ratio. For bikes with a skimmed head, Norton introduced a 2mm thick alloy head gasket, which reduced the CR to around 8.8:1, but could spread and catch the pushrods in their tunnel. A permanent cure was found with the RH5 head, which retained the Combat's 32mm ports but was not skimmed, giving a 8.9:1 compression ratio, and the RH6 head, which gave 9.5:1 and was specified as an option for the Roadster only. A new head gasket was also introduced, a Hallite composite design with steel inlets around the bores. This type of gasket was very good at fixing the oil leaks that the solid copper and aluminium gaskets tended to allow. Norton spent a lot of time and effort on fixing the problems introduced by the Combat motor, and the public seemed to appreciate this, since sales continued. The bike numbering system took a real battering at this time as engines were built, held in stock, modified and shipped, and all order was lost.

Despite the turmoil caused by the Combat engine fiasco, development continued and the opportunity was taken to add an electric start to the motor to help it compete with the Japanese opposition. This was not Norton's first foray into electric starting: the Norton Electra, a 384cc development of the 349cc Navigator, was produced with a Lucas M3 starter motor that drove the crankshaft via epicyclic gear train and a single strand chain. By all accounts the Electra mechanism worked but needed a well-charged battery. The Commando system placed the starter motor, an American Prestolite unit (finally seen on the Mark 3 model in 1975) in the old magneto position behind the barrels, bolted to the crankcase extension. The motor drove the engine using a chain to the intermediate gear. The prototype installation would start the engine, but was not mechanically robust. The mechanism was very sensitive to changes in timing and a kickback from the engine could destroy the timing gears and, in extreme cases, would break the timing side crankcase casting. The mechanism was

dropped after that happened during a demonstration of the prototype to Dennis Poore.

The growth of the Commando engine to 828cc for the 1973 season was intended to improve both reliability and rideability, and was not intended to increase performance over that of the 750cc unit. To achieve both these aims the bottom end was strengthened and the state of tune of the engine was lower than the 750's, mainly achieved by lowering the compression ratio. The increase in capacity was arrived at by increasing the bore to 77mm while retaining the stroke of 89mm, giving a capacity of 828cc (50 cu in) while the compression ratio was reduced to a more conservative 8.5:1. The unit gave a claimed 60bhp at 5,800rpm, the same as the post-Combat 9:1 750 unit output of 60bhp at 6,800rpm.

Actual engine modifications were extensive. The crankcases were strengthened and the new barrel, still in cast iron, was fixed to the barrel with a combination of five studs (three at the front and two at the back) through the cylinder flange and four through bolts, two on each side. The through bolts were positioned each side of the spark plugs, passed through the head and barrel and then screwed into holes in the crankcases, which had reinforced threads using helicoil inserts. This meant there was a lot more metal on the barrel, increasing its strength and rigidity, and also helped to stiffen up the head/barrel/crankcase assembly. It also makes it easy to identify an 828cc unit as there is no flange on the side of the barrel – just a large oblong casting below the fins through which the bolts run. The revised crankcases also regained the sump plug in the rear of the cases with its gauze filter, as previously seen on the 750s up to 1971, along with improvements to the oil pick-up area to improve scavenging. The crank was still a bolt-up three-piece unit as on the 750, but came in for some modifications with a reshaped flywheel to compensate for the heavier 850 pistons and retain the 52 per cent balance factor carried over from the 750, and the crank was bolted up using six studs and nuts, rather than the 750cc unit's combination of four studs and two bolts. Finally, FAG Superblend tapered roller main

The outer four head fixings, two on each side, bolt through the head and barrels into the crankcases on the 850 unit.

bearings were fitted as standard. All these improvements made for a strong and reliable unit, which produced loads of low-down torque and was very flexible. Along with the reintroduced sump plug scavenge filter, the 850 models also had a full flow car type cartridge oil filter placed in the return side to the oil tank: this arrangement was probably the best oil filtration system seen on any British bike at the time.

The special 750cc production racer engine produced alongside the 828cc unit in 1973 retained the 850's 77mm bore but had a reduced stroke of 80mm. Sporting a black painted barrel, the engine retained all the 850 unit's improvements including the bolt-through 850-type barrel and was extensively tuned. The engines had a 4-S camshaft, revised valve angles, larger inlet valves, hidural exhaust valve guides, forged steel connecting rods, 10.5:1 compression pistons with solid skirts and Lucas Rita optically triggered electronic ignition. When fitted with the optional 33mm carburettors, bell mouth inlets and an open megaphone exhaust, Norton claimed 80bhp.

Commando Numbers

Unlike Triumph and BSA at the time, Norton did not have well-defined model years and tended to introduce changes and new models at random times throughout the year. The Commando was identified by its engine and frame numbers, which matched until the introduction of the Mark 3 models in 1975, when the engine number ran from 325,001 and the frame numbers ran from F125001. Until January 1972 Norton policy was to have a consecutive run of engine numbers, but then the policy was changed, with the numbers starting from 200,001. A new range of numbers was introduced with the 828cc engine in April 1973, with the new engine starting at 300,000. The Combat engine debacle also caused chaos to the dating of the numbering system as engines were pulled from bikes already on the production line in order to replace their main bearings. In addition, unlike Triumph and BSA, the individual models that made up the Commando range did not have any identifiers incorporated in the engine/frame numbers, so it is impossible to determine from the number alone what model a bike was originally.

There are reasonably well-documented numbers at which significant model changes occurred, and these are reproduced in the accompanying table, along with manufacturing dates of specific numbers. They have been derived from various sources, including the Norvil parts catalogue, Roy Bacon's *Norton Twin Restoration*, Jeff Clew's 'Norton Commando Super Profile', Rebekka Smith's article 'Norton Commando 750 & 850' published in the November 1995 issue of *British Bike*, the Norton Owners Club (NOC, which used the original factory records) and original Norton literature. They have been checked against various online sources, including the Norton Owners Club. As with all British bike numbering systems, however, there is often conflicting or wrong data, so the author makes no claims as to the accuracy of these numbers.

Sample Commando Numbers

Engine number	Approx. date	Notes and source
126,125	Feb 1968	First Commando production model (also in *British Bike*, Nov 1995)
128,646	Sept 1968	*British Bike*, Nov 1995
129,125	Late 1968	New frame with headstock gusset replaced with second top tube to prevent breakage
129,145	Nov 1968	*British Bike*, Nov 1995
131,180	March 1969	Fastback name introduced (also in *British Bike*, Nov 1995)
131,257	March 1969	First 'S' type: new crankcases with points driven from end of camshaft and inboard tacho drive. Last 'S' type was 135,088. (NB Fastback did not receive new crankcases until engine number 133,668)
133,668	Sept 1969	*British Bike*, Nov 1995
134,108	Sept 1969[?]	First engine produced at Wolverhampton. (NB engines with a 'P' suffix were produced at Wolverhampton)
134,000	Jan 1970	NOC date
135,088	March 1970	Last 'S' type (from Jerry Doe's 'Norton Commando Forum')
135,140	March 1970	First Roadster model (also in *British Bike*, Nov 1995)
139,571	Sept 1970	Fastback Mark 2 (last 141,717) (also in *British Bike*, Nov 1995)
141,900	Jan 1970	NOC (last 1970 bike 150,500)
141,717	Jan 1971	*British Bike*, Nov 1995
141,783	Jan 1971	Fastback Mark 3

Engine number	Approx. date	Notes and source
142,534	Jan 1971	Roadster Mark 2 (also in *British Bike*, Nov 1995)
145,234	Mar 1971	SS (last SS 150,723, Oct 1971) (also in *British Bike*, Nov 1995)
144,343[?]	April 1971	Fastback LR
146,074	May 1971	Hi-Rider (also in *British Bike*, Nov 1995)
149,194	June 1971	From data plate of individual machine
150,723	Oct 1971	*British Bike*, Nov 1995. (NB this number is higher than the NOC's last 1971 bike)
200,001	Jan 1972	Previous engine numbering system abandoned. New models introduced as Fastback Mark 4, Fastback Mark 4 LR, Roadster Mark 4, Hi-Rider Mark 4 (also in *British Bike*, Nov 1995)
200,976		First Combat engine
212,278	March 1972	Interstate introduced
211,110[?]	Sept 1972	First 'de-tuned' (i.e. non-Combat) engine with revised cylinder head giving lower compression ratio. (NB numbering during 1972 was not very sequential)
212,173	Sept 1972	New composite head gasket
220,000	March 1973	Roadster Mark 5, High-Rider Mark 5, Interstate Mark 5 (also in *British Bike*, Nov 1995)
230,558	June 1973	NOC
230,571	Sept 1973	NOC
230,935	Oct 1973	Last 750cc model (NOC)
300,000	April 1973	First 850cc models (also in *British Bike*, Nov 1995)
300,200	March 1973	First 850cc models (NOC)
306,591	Sept 1973	850cc Mark 1A models (also in *British Bike*, Nov 1995)
307,311	Jan 1974	850cc Mark 2 and Mark 2A models
310,360	Dec 1973	850cc, NOC
316,600	June 1974	850cc, NOC
325,001	Feb 1975	First 850 Mark 3. Frame numbers no longer match the engine and start at F125001
326,000	Dec 1974	850cc, NOC
333,000	June 1975	850cc, NOC
335,400	1977	850cc, NOC
336,538	Last known,	NOC

Oddities are still emerging: recent posts on the Jerry Doe AccessNorton website, for example, claim that some 850 models have been positively identified as having numbers around 235xxx.

Carburation

Commando carburation was relatively straightforward. The production bikes were all equipped with the Amal Concentric instrument in various choke sizes, a simple and easily tuned carburettor that was the industry standard at the time. Its design was simple and driven mainly by unit cost: it was introduced at the insistence of the main British manufacturers to provide a cheaper and easier to produce replacement for the earlier and more complex Monobloc design. Its main design feature was the float, which was positioned concentric to the main jet holder – hence its name. This meant that not only was the carburettor less sensitive to lean angles and acceleration forces than the Monobloc, with its float chamber positioned on its side, but also that one casing could be used to provide a left- or right-handed unit when suitably drilled. The only external adjusters were a throttle stop, pilot jet screw and tickler (to flood the float chamber for starting), and these could be positioned on either side of the carburettor body depending on the drilling of the main casting.

The device had a cable-operated slide and needle to control the main jet, and a pilot system that bypassed the main jet for small throttle openings and tick-over. The choke mechanism was a simple cable-operated air slide located within the main slide, which blocked off about 50 per cent of the air passage through the main choke when used. The only downside was the need to keep the cost of the instrument down, resulting in Amal casting the main parts of the carburettor in a poor performing alloy, resulting in relatively rapid wear, especially between the slide and the carburettor body. This leads to problems in setting the carburettor up and makes it difficult to maintain a decent state of tune.

The first Commandos were equipped with 930 units: these were 900 Series 30mm choke units, both left- and right-handed, and they continued to be specified until the Combat motor of 1972, when 932 units with 32mm chokes were specified. The 828cc Commando continued with 32mm units until the end of production.

The twin Amal Concentric carbs are bolted onto parallel manifolds. A balance pipe connects the two inlets to make a smoother tick-over, and rubber bellows connect the carbs to the air box.

Gearbox and Primary Drive

The Commando retained a separate four-speed gearbox throughout its life. It was based closely on the box used in the Atlas and was renowned for having easy shifting characteristics. The gearbox was a conventional British design, with a main shaft and layshaft and a direct-drive top gear. There were four pairs of gears on the main and layshafts, with a sliding gear on each shaft that was moved by selector forks controlled by tracks in a rotating cam plate.

The cam plate was operated from the gear pedal by a positive stop mechanism and was positioned using a sprung loader plunger. Power was fed into the mainshaft via the clutch and was directed through the relevant pair of gears, emerging at the final drive sprocket that was fixed to a sleeve gear on the mainshaft and was positioned behind the clutch and inner chain case. Drive was taken to the back wheel by chain. The box was mounted in the rear engine plates, and pivoted around the bottom bolt to provide adjustment to the primary chain: on the Mark 3, however, the gearbox was fixed in position. The right-hand side gear shift pattern was one up, and three down (the reverse of what was becoming the industry norm). This was changed to one down and three up with the Mark 3, when the gear change pedal was moved to the drive side. The gearbox has a good reputation, but it was originally designed for a 30bhp 500cc twin and so it can be overworked in an 850cc twin. The layshaft bearing on the drive side of the case tends to fail: symptoms include roughness in the intermediate gears and the kick-start pedal rotating downwards when the bike is running.

The Commando primary drive was conventional in layout, with a triplex primary chain driven from the engine sprocket, and a multi-plate clutch fixed on the gearbox mainshaft. The clutch design was a departure from the British industry norm. Recognizing that the standard three or four spring multi-plate clutches used on most British twins in the 1960s would struggle to cope with the torque and power of the Commando engine, Norton went outside the bike industry to automotive clutch specialists Laycock de Normanville, who designed a new four friction plate diaphragm spring unit that could

The AMC gearbox is pretty reliable, but the layshaft bearing can fail. It has a one up, three down shift pattern as standard.

The gearbox is pivoted on its lower mount to adjust the primary chain. A block and screw mechanism on the top fixing is used to lock the box in position.

The Commando primary drive has a triple (three row) chain and a diaphragm spring clutch.

The Mark 3 had a left-foot gear change and a new primary chain case, which was fixed in place with ten screws around its periphery.

cope with the power without giving too heavy an action at the handlebar lever. In addition to the spring strength, the single large spring meant even pressure across the surface of the clutch, making it easy to set up.

The primary chain was adjusted in the traditional British way by moving the gearbox on a pivot on the underside, changing the distance between the clutch and the crankshaft. This meant there was an oil seal in the inner primary chain case, which had to be mounted on a sliding steel fixture: as this fitting wore it gave potential for oil leaks. The outer primary chain case was fixed to the inner by a single central bolt, with a flexible rubber ring in a groove to keep the oil in. This was another potential source of oil leaks, especially if the spacers on the rear of the fixing pillar were wrongly positioned or the cases were bowed. In practice, however, the system worked well as both inner and outer cases were thick and rigid alloy castings. The clutch and basic layout remained the same throughout the range, but the introduction of the electric start Mark 3 led to a number of changes. As the shaft for the left-foot gear change on the Mark 3 now passed through the centre of the chain case, the cases needed to be modified and NVT replaced the central mounting bolt with ten screws around the periphery of the case. The new gear change mechanism was simple in concept. The original gear change shaft was reversed and lengthened, forming a cross shaft that ran between the gearbox and engine cases into the chain case, where it was supported on a bush in the inner case. A small gear wheel was splined onto the end of the shaft.

A spindle was mounted on a bush on the outer case, with a gear to engage with the cross shaft and splines to carry the gear lever on the outside. Hence moving the lever on the outside of the case transmitted the movement via the cross shaft to the original gear shift mechanism. The electric start was mounted on the top of the inner chain case on a semicircular protrusion, and was held in place with two screws. The electric starter drove the crankshaft though a chain of gears and a mechanical sprag clutch to transfer the drive from the starter motor to the crank. The gear train also featured a spring-loaded clutch to protect against

kickbacks or backfires. As the left-foot gear change meant that the gearbox could no longer be moved to adjust the primary chain, the final modification in the chain case was the introduction of a hydraulic primary chain tensioner. This was mounted in front of the clutch and comprised two spring-loaded plungers that pressed against the top and bottom runs of the triplex primary chain. Pressure in the tensioner was maintained by the springs, and the correct tension was maintained automatically by a set level of primary chain case oil in the tensioner. All in all the Mark 3 had a series of major changes in comparison to the previous simple system.

Isolastic System

The most innovative feature of the Commando was the Isolatic system. Derived from the words 'isolate' and 'elastic', the system addressed one of the main problems faced by the vertical twins being produced by the British industry: user discomfort caused by vibration. The Isolastic system was invented by Norton's chief development engineer, Bernard Hooper, and was developed into production by Hooper and Bob Trigg, another Norton engineer. The system was not an ideal engineering solution to the vibration problem of big vertical twins, as it did not solve the fundamental problems of vibration: a Commando engine still vibrates, but it was a cost-effective and timely means of isolating the rider from the effects of the vibration.

The Commando engine has both its pistons going up and down at the same time, and firing on alternate strokes. This gives smooth power pulses, but generates a lot of primary imbalance as the pistons 'push' up and down, making the engine try to jump up and down, and giving rise to vibration in the vertical plane. The alternating power pulses also add a rocking motion, making the engine shake from side to side and giving vibration in the horizontal plane, but in the Commando's case this is not as great as the up-and-down movement. In order to isolate the rider from this vibration, any system has to absorb both the up-and-down (vertical) and side-to-side (horizontal) movement.

The Isolastic System and Previous Attempts at Rubber Mounting

There were two other notable attempts to use rubber mountings to isolate the rider from a vertical twin's vibes: the 1950s Sunbeam S7/S8 range, produced by BSA, and the 1980s Triumph.

The Sunbeam S7 was introduced in 1947 and was produced along with the S8 until 1956. The Sunbeam was a 500cc parallel twin mounted longitudinally. Rubber mounting was introduced very late in its development cycle (or early in the production cycle, depending on how you look at it) when the vibration levels of the pre-production versions of the twin were found to be unacceptable.

The engine and gearbox construction was much like a very car's, being bolted together with a single plate clutch placed between them in a bell housing. The rubber mounting was achieved using rubber block mounts on the front and rear of the engine and gearbox unit. With the final drive being by shaft, a 'Layrub' universal joint connected the gearbox output to the drive shaft and with its built-in rubber bushing could handle both the engine and gearbox unit's movement and the rear suspension movement. Technically the overall package was successful, managing to isolate much of the engine vibration from the rider, but the Sunbeam was never successful commercially as it was aimed at the somewhat limited 'Gentleman's Tourer' market and production ceased in 1956.

The Triumph Co-operative at Meriden started to look into measures against vibration in the late 1970s and obviously looked closely at Norton's successful Isolastic system. This, however, was covered by a number of patents owned by Norton Villiers Triumph and the Co-op had to find a system that did not infringe them. Help came from Bernard Hooper, Norton's former head development engineer, who left Norton in 1975 and set up as Bernard Hooper Engineering Ltd, where he designed System 360, an anti-vibration system for motorcycles that did not infringe any Norton patents and intended to be as far as possible maintenance-free. The system used rubber blocks, rather than the Norton's tubular mounts, and mounted the engine at three points: at the cylinder head, under the crankcases and at the back of the gearbox. The head and crankcase mounts used bonded rubber mouldings and pressed steel mounts to isolate the engine from the frame. The rear mount had to preserve the chain line and tension, and comprised two new engine plates, which bolted directly onto the back of the engine unit at the gearbox and primary chain case. These plates carried the swinging arm pivot, so the swinging arm was attached rigidly to the engine unit. A second spindle was positioned below the swinging arm spindle and was attached to each end of the swing arm spindle using vertical arms. This arrangement allowed the swing arm to move in a controlled manner in an arc around the lower pivot, giving enough slight fore and aft movement enough to take up the movement allowed by two rubber mounts, and was intended keep the chain tension and alignment within acceptable limits, while still allowing full suspension travel.

The design allowed the whole engine and swinging arm assembly to rock up and down independently of the frame while pivoting on the secondary rear spindle. This meant that the vibration in the up and down plane (the plane in which the Triumph's engine vibrated the most) could be accommodated by the rubber mounts while the swinging arm pivot (and the whole rear of the engine unit) could not move from side to side, hence preserving wheel alignment and handling. Anecdotal evidence, however, shows that this aim was not necessarily met, with the owner of one machine having to install a trials type chain tensioner to stop the chain jumping off the sprockets. The system gave Triumph a system that could, with further development to address the chain tension issues, have resulted in a bike that was acceptable to the police and other fleet users of motorcycles.

Experiments at the factory using accelerometers to measure vibration at the footrests, handlebars and seat showed a significant overall reduction of approximately 60 per cent between a standard bike and an AV framed example, and gave a major improvement to rider comfort, especially at higher speeds. The AV frames were codenamed 'Enforcer', another pointer to the police market at which the bike was aimed.

The factory plan was to introduce the AV frame in the 1983 season, but Meriden stopped production and closed before the system could be put into production. A total of just forty-three AV models were built, a sad end to a promising design.

The Sunbeam S7 featured a rubber-mounted engine and was relatively successful as a 'Gentleman's Tourer'.

The Triumph system used rubber blocks to avoid infringing on the Norton Isolastic patents.

In the early 1980s Triumph almost got a Bonneville into production with a rubber-mounted engine.

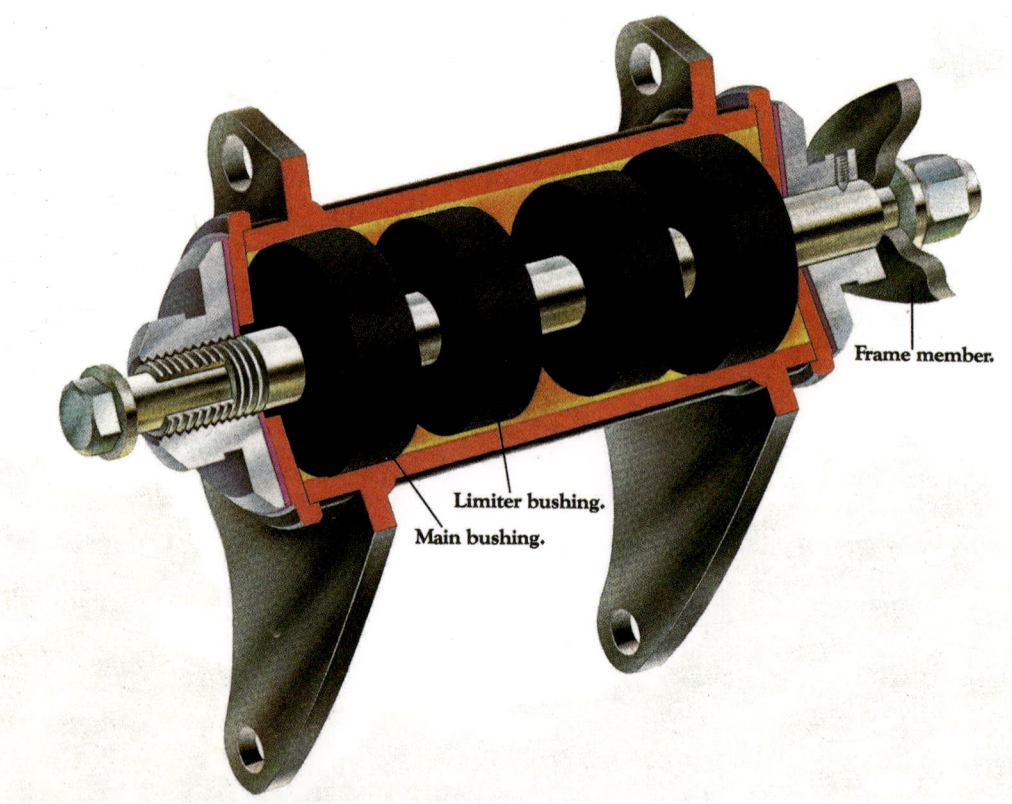

Frame member.

Limiter bushing.

Main bushing.

The Isolastic system had rubber mounts encased in tubular mounts. The larger diameter ones
allowed the engine to move up and down, and the smaller ones acted as buffers to limit movement.
Sideways play was limited by a plastic bush between the inner and outer end plates.

Rubber mounting of the engine can be used to isolate the rider from these vibrations, but this gives rise to another pair of problems on a chain drive motorcycle. The alignment of the drive sprocket on the engine/gearbox and the driven sprocket on the rear wheel must be maintained to pretty close tolerances to keep the chain from jumping off the sprockets, and there must not be too much movement of the engine/gearbox relative to the rear wheel to maintain chain tension. While a shaft drive can handle some movement of the engine and gearbox proportional to the wheel, even minor misalignment of a chain drive will lead to excessive wear and potential failure; the chain will come off the sprockets or could even break. If the rear wheel is rigidly fixed to the engine and gearbox to maintain chain alignment, there would be too much movement of the rear wheel relative to the front wheel, causing handling problems.

The breakthrough that made the Isolastic system possible was the realization that if the movement of the engine could be limited in the horizontal plane, then the rear wheel could be rigidly mounted to the engine and gearbox without affecting the handling. This was a viable approach as most of the vibration produced by the engine was in the vertical plane. Hooper and Trigg set out to design a workable system. The gearbox was bolted top and bottom to a pair of plates, which were bolted to the rear of the engine cases, making a strong and rigid unit. The gearbox could pivot on the bottom mount to allow for primary chain adjustment. There were two steel tubes welded between the two plates, one on the top and one at the rear. The swinging arm pivoted on the rear one, while the top one was used to mount the unit in the frame. A second tube was bolted to the front of the engine, providing a second mounting point. These front and top mounting tubes carried the Isolastic rubbers, the centres of which were attached to the frame by long studs. The outer tube could bounce up and down on the rubbers, isolating the frame from the vibration. There were two types of rubber: the main bushes that filled the gap between the central stud and the tube, and smaller diameter limiter bushes that acted as extra bushing when excessive movement occurred. The bushes soaked up the vertical movement, and horizontal movement was catered for by careful shimming of the end of the tube relative to the frame. On each side of the tube there was an inner collar with a large diameter hole that fitted over the inner stud and allowed for movement of the tube relative to the stud. A second collar was fitted onto the stud and a polyurethane washer was fitted between the two collars to give a smooth bearing as the collars moved relative to each other. The inner collar had provision for shims to be placed between it and the tube to take up any horizontal movement. The final engine mount was the head steady, which used two rubber cotton reel mounts (also used as Austin Mini exhaust mounts) to soak up both horizontal and vertical movement.

The system worked well, and was widely acclaimed by the press, although the shimming system for adjustment, which was fiddly and time consuming to set up correctly, was not liked. Badly shimmed frames could and did lead to errant handling, and there are many tales of poor handling Commandos because of this. It was only when the Mark 3 Commando was introduced that the labour-intensive shimming was relegated to history. The original patent had included a 'vernier' adjustment mechanism, but this was not incorporated on the bikes as it was deemed to cost too much. The adjustment system meant that the outer collar was threaded onto the inner stud, and could be screwed in or out to set the required clearance, making adjustments quick and easy, with no need for any shims.

Frame and Swinging Arm

Due to the Isolastic mounts isolating the frame from the engine vibration, it was possible for the Commando frame to be a lightweight design that concentrated on the essentials of providing excellent handling and road holding. The frame comprised a 2¼in (5.7cm) 16 gauge large diameter tube, which formed a backbone that ran from the steering head back to the level of the rear shock

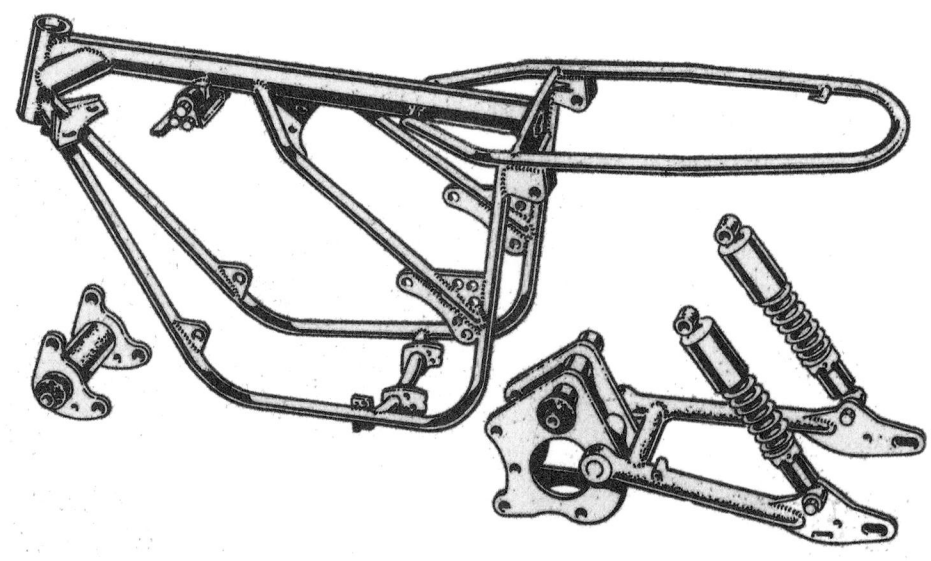

If your frame looks like this it belongs in a museum, not on the road. The inadequate front gusset sets up stress that makes the down tubes break just below the steering head.

This is the later frame (actually a 1971 item), which has the small secondary tube under the main spine. This gives it strength and it does not suffer breakage.

absorber top mounts. A bracing plate was welded to the rear end of the tube to join the rear shock absorber top mounts to the main backbone. At the front of the main backbone, a tubular head-stock was welded in place along with a sheet metal gusset to form the steering head. From the steering head, two 1in (2.54cm) diameter tubes ran down in front of the engine, under the crankcases and back up to each side of the rear bracing plate, forming an unstressed cradle to carry the engine and gearbox. A pair of 1in (2.54cm) diameter bracing tubes ran diagonally upwards from the back of this each side of the cradle to the middle of the top tube, triangulating the structure and providing most of the frame's torsional rigidity. Finally there was a rear loop made out of 1in diameter tube, designed to support the seat and rear mudguard. The front of the loop was fixed to each side of the main back-

bone, roughly halfway between the bracing plate and the two bracing tubes, and ran back through the bracing plate across the top of the shock absorber top mounts and formed a loop around the rear of the frame that followed the line of the seat. The frame weighed a mere 24lb (10.8kg) and as such was a truly lightweight design.

The first major change to the frame was the strengthening of the steering head. Once the first bikes were being sold, a number of frames were found to have fractures between the front down tubes and the steering head around the 'U' shaped strengthening gusset. The fractures were caused by a combination of poor handling of crated bikes shock-loading the steering head and stress concentrations in the steering head. Ken Sprayson of Reynolds had predicted that the frame would break there and proposed a simple and elegant solution, running an additional small diameter tube from the bottom of the steering head back to the middle of the existing top tube where the rear bracing struts were fixed. When tested on the infamous paved surface at the Chobham test track, Spayson's fix survived while two frames made to test Norton's fixes, a top tube made of heavier gauge tubing and increased gusseting, both failed. This modification, however, does make it awkward to fit the cylinder head to the motor while in the frame, as it significantly reduces the clearance between the head and the frame.

The other major modification made to the frame was carried out in 1971 at engine number 141783 when the centre stand was shifted to the engine plates. The modification comprised a cradle with centre stand fixings and a new stiffening bar, placed between the two frame down tubes underneath the crankcases. This replaced the bar that was positioned further back on the frame tubes under the gearbox and which carried the original centre stand lugs. The side stand was fixed to a pin on the drive side by this tube, and was retained by a circlip. This fixing was used for 1971 only, since the stand reduced clearance and the circlip failed; this could result in the side stand falling off and fouling the rear wheel with dangerous results for the rider. The side stand location was changed to a conventional lug and bolt fixing for 1972. The frame head angle was reduced from 63 degrees to 62 degrees with the introduction of the 850 model in April 1973, with the fork yokes modified to maintain the same wheelbase as the 750.

Frame production was carried out in Italy from around 1973: frames for the 850 Mark 2 were certainly Italian, identified by an 'F' prefix to the frame number.

The swinging arm was a tubular affair with bracing around the pivot. It ran on two flanged solid bushes that pivoted on a hollow steel pin tightly fitted in the tube that joined the two halves of the rear engine/gearbox cradle. The pin was located in the tube with a single ½in bolt, and this less than positive locating mechanism was eventually changed to twin cotter pins on late Mark 2 and all the Mark 3 850s. The pivot bushes need to be lubricated with oil not grease, but

Norton provided a grease nipple on one end of the pivot to confuse the local mechanics. Use of grease will result in rapid wear. Oil injected into the shaft was kept in place by a system of end caps and wicks.

Front and Rear Suspension

The Commando used the famous Norton 'Roadholder' forks throughout its life, and gave a reasonable 6in (15.2cm) suspension movement. The forks were hydraulically damped on compression and rebound, using internal springs. Chromed stanchions were carried in cast iron yokes (triple trees in American usage) and these initially pivoted on separate ball races holding eighteen loose ball bearings top and bottom. This arrangement was superseded by a pair of ball

The front forks are the famous Norton Roadholders, with internal springs, chromed legs and light alloy sliders. Iron yokes (or triple trees) have the instrument cup bolted onto them using the stanchion top nuts.

The disc brake was introduced in 1972 and was an improvement on the TLS drum. The calliper was unique to Norton, but was made by Lockheed.

races and a spacer in early 1971 at frame number 141783. The fork sliders or legs were made of aluminium, so were light, and were polished to look good from the start. The use of aluminium also cut down on unsprung weight (in contrast to Triumph and BSA's continuing use of steel sliders up to 1971), which helped the forks to perform. Each fork leg took 150cc (5 fluid oz) of fork oil. The internal damping mechanism comprised a damper rod fixed to the top nut and a damper tube bolted to the bottom of the fork slider. As the slider moved up and down, the oil in the fork restricts the relative movement of the tube and rod as it is forced between the two components in such a way as to provide optimum damping to control the movement of the front wheel. The fork remained pretty much unchanged throughout the life of the Commando. The original Fast-

backs came with steel shrouds to provide protection to the stanchions. These were replaced with sportier rubber bellows on later models – or discarded altogether on US models, where a small rubber dust excluder at the top of the slider did its inadequate best to prevent premature bush wear, but the exposed chrome fork legs looked really good.

The main changes to the front forks came in 1972, with the introduction of the disc brake, when the right-hand side fork slider was modified with cast-in lugs to carry the calliper behind the fork leg.

In 1975 the Mark 3 reversed the position of the disc calliper, placing it in front of the left-hand side leg. To achieve this NVT simply swapped the fork sliders and the front wheel around.

The rear suspension used oil damped Girling units, which were angled about 30 degrees from the vertical. This was unusual on British bikes at the time, but gave greater rear wheel movement for a given suspension unit. This helped to give the comfortable ride that the Commando is renowned for. Like the front forks, the dampers started off with steel shrouds. These were chromed and covered the top half of the spring providing a reasonable compromise between sporty looks and weather protection, but for 1971 the shrouds had vanished, leaving the chromed spring and damper rod exposed to the elements.

Brakes and Wheels

The Commando road models started with a twin leading-shoe front brake, which was improved and then replaced with a single disc brake. The initial models sported a new design of twin leading-shoe, 8in diameter brake housed in the Norton full-width alloy hub. The brake followed contemporary British brake design practice with an alloy brake plate, with external operating arms linked by an adjustable tie rod, and was a good performer well, if not as good as the equivalent BSA/Triumph unit. The unit had an air scoop in the front to provide extra cooling, and a set of three 1in (2.5cm) diameter holes at the rear of the brake plate to let the hot air out. Both the air scoop and the extractor holes had a fine wire gauze covering to keep the local insect population out of the brake, and both could be equipped with an optional blanking plate for temperate climates to prevent too much cooling.

The main failing of the brake was flex in the brake plate, which lost braking efficiency. This was addressed for 1972 with a stiffening kit, which added a steel plate behind the brake shoes that mounted on the ends of the brake cams and pivots and supported the whole structure. Kits are available to retro-fit the plate to earlier TLS brakes.

The hydraulically operated front disc brake was introduced for the 1972 model year: it was initially standard on the Interstate and an option on the other bikes in the range. It was rapidly standardized across the range and was offered as a

The 1968–71 front brake was a twin leading shoe unit with air scoop and round extractor holes. The front scoop was blanked off with an alloy plate as standard in the UK, as the factory thought the brake did not need it for road use.

Up to the Mark 3 the rear brake was a cable-operated 7in single leading shoe unit.

The Mark 3 had its front disc moved to the left-hand side with the calliper mounted ahead of the slider.

The Mark 3 for 1975 gained a disc rear brake, hydraulically operated from the new left-hand brake pedal.

retro-fit for earlier bikes. By 1973 the Norton disc brake was standardized on the Interstate, Roadster and Interpol, with only the Hi-Rider still fitted with the twin leading-shoe drum as standard. The disc brake was developed jointly by Lockheed and Norton, and was completely different to the contemporary Triumph Lockheed unit. The brake disc was a chrome-plated cast iron, 10.7in (270 cm) diameter unit mounted directly onto a small alloy 'cotton reel' hub with five high tensile studs and nuts. The calliper bolted directly onto a new cast-in lug on the rear of the right-hand side fork slider. The calliper was an alloy casing with cast-in cooling 'fins' on its top, which were really more of a styling feature, and used round brake pads unique to Norton. The brake was welcomed at the time of its introduction, but even then the magazine tests felt that it was a bit wooden in feel, but provided a significant improvement on the TLS drum brake. The master cylinder fitted to the handlebar had an alloy reservoir with a smart polished alloy cap, unlike Triumph's plastic capped unit, although a black plastic cap was introduced for the Mark 3 in 1975. The standard Lucas switchgear bolted straight onto the master cylinder's rear face, and was operated by a high quality forged alloy lever, again in contrast to the Triumph's tacky pressed steel chromed lever.

The rear brake on the Commando was a 7in cable-operated unit on the whole range up to the Mark 3. The cast iron rear brake drum was separate from the rear hub, and also carried the chain drive sprocket.

The light alloy rear hub was attached to the brake drum initially with three studs, allowing the rear wheel to be removed once the spindle, speedo drive and the three studs were removed without disturbing the chain or brake. This was modified for 1971 by discarding the bolts and locating the wheel onto the brake hub with three vanes, incorporating rubber shock absorbers. To remove this wheel, the rider just had to remove the wheel spindle, speedo drive and a spacer, making the wheel truly quickly detachable.

The Mark 3 front disc calliper was moved to the front of the fork slider and changed sides at the same time. This apparently meaningless change was to get rid of a slight instability caused by the calliper when positioned behind the fork leg. The front hub was changed at the same time to incorporate a circlip to retain the front wheel bearing retaining washer and prevent it from undoing: it is very dangerous to simply swap the fork legs over and reverse the front wheel on a pre-Mark 3 bike, since the bearing retaining washer can undo with potentially disastrous consequences for the rider.

The Mark 3 also saw the introduction of a rear disc brake. This was heralded at the time as an improvement to increase stopping power and reduce unsprung weight, which it was, but it was also easier to engineer a hydraulically operated disc brake using the same components as the front brake with the transposition of the gear change and rear brake pedals. The brake used an identical disc and calliper casting to those used on the front, and an all-new conical hub that was needed to provide clearance for the disc calliper. The rear drive sprocket was driven from the hub via a five vane rubber cush drive, and the wheel retained the quickly detachable feature of the earlier hub, in so

much as the rear chain did not need to be disturbed to remove the wheel. The calliper was carried on a large mounting plate, which was located on the axle and the rear suspension mount bolt, and could be moved out of the way to assist in the removal of the QD wheel. A hook was provided to hang the calliper on the rear frame rail below the seat. The master cylinder was bolted inside the right-hand side footrest carrier along with the fluid reservoir, where it was neatly tucked in and protected in case of a spill. A short chromed pedal pivoted on an extension above the footrest to complete the ensemble. With the introduction of the Mark 3 alongside the T160 Trident, it was strange that NVT did not rationalize their disk brake to one type: both the Triumph and Norton unit were manufactured by Lockheed, so this must represent a lost opportunity for making some economies of scale.

Tinware

Tinware is a bit of a misnomer in the case of the Commando, as for the first years of production glass fibre was used instead of the traditional pressed steel for fuel tanks and side panels, as well

The Roadster side panel was also used on the Hi-Rider. It is a lot smaller than the previous Fastbacks or the later Interstate.

In contrast to the other 750 Commandos, the 1970 'S' type and Roadster placed the oil tank to the front of the battery carrier, with the battery situated behind it.

The Interstate tank (left) is significantly wider and longer than the Roadster's.

as the fastback tail unit and even the standard roadster rear light fairing. In contrast to other manufacturers, Norton minimized the use of bracketry, and the main piece of 'internal' metalwork combined the battery carrier and air filter into a single simple unit fitted alongside the oil tank. In fact, on early fastback Commandos the outer side of the oil tank was used as the right-hand side panel, and this dictated the shape of the left-hand panel.

The 'S' type was the first model to use the abbreviated triangular side panels, the front edge of which followed the line of the frame bracing tube that ran from the seat nose down to the 'Z' plate. These were initially glass fibre, the right-hand side bolting onto the top of the oil tank and the left-hand side locating on two rubber-mounted pins on its rear edge and held in position by a Dzus fastener on the top front edge. Some of these panels had a moulded-in tray for the tool kit, some didn't.

A pressed steel tray was located on the rear engine mounts and supported the oil tank on the timing side, with the battery on the timing side and the rear plate of the air cleaner housing at its front. The 'S' type and first year Roadster used a different tray, with the oil tank carried at the front and the battery at the rear.

One of the defining elements of any Commando is its fuel tank. The Commando fuel tanks came in a number of styles, the small Roadster, the large capacity Interstate, the small off-road/chopper style used on the Hi-Rider and SS, the initial medium capacity Fastback and the larger capacity Fastback LR unit, based on the Interpol.

All the Commando tanks were made initially in glass fibre, and the colour and 'metalflake' finishes could be impregnated into the gel coat, which meant the item did not require painting after moulding. Some of the early 1970s Commando metalflake finishes were quite spectacular and unlike anything seen before on a production bike. However, the UK introduced a ban on the use of the material for fuel tanks in 1973. Both steel and glass fibre tanks were still offered on the US market during 1973, with only steel tanks offered in all markets by 1974. Note that the Interpol (and the LR) always had a steel tank, as

Norton Fuel Tanks

Model	Year	Material	Capacity imp gal	US gal	ltr
20M3/Fastback	1968–72	Glass fibre	3.25	3.9	14.7
Fastback LR	1971–72	Steel	4.0	4.7	17.7
'R' Type	1969	Glass fibre	2.25	2.7	10.1
SS/Hi-Rider	1970	Glass fibre	2	2.3	9
Hi-Rider	?	Steel	2	2.25	9
Roadster	1970	Glass fibre	2.25	2.7	
Roadster	1972	Steel	2.5	3	11
Roadster 850	1972	Steel	2.5	3	11
Interstate	1972	Glass fibre	5.2	6.25	23.5
Interstate	1972	Steel	5.4	6.5	24.5
Interstate 850	1972	Steel	4.8	5.75	21.6
Interstate Mk3	1975	Steel	5.25	6.3	24
JPN		Steel (with glass fibre cover)	3.0	3.5	13.6
Interpol	1972	Steel (with radio insert)	3.5	4.25	16
Interpol	1972	Steel (without radio insert)	4.0	4.75	18

this was one of the UK police requirements. The production racer tanks for track use were always made in glass fibre. This means that there are a large number of versions of the Commando fuel tank, and the accompanying table identifies these variations. All data is taken from the official Norton brochures, but even these figures should be treated with caution as there appear to be some discrepancies.

One distinguishing feature that Norton utilized was the use of pin striping on the tanks and side panels to indicate engine size: the 750 Commandos had single pinstripes on their tanks and side panels, while the 850 models had two (one wide, one narrow).

Electrics

All Commando electrics were 12 volt, positive earth systems with coil ignition and solid state Zener diode voltage regulation, with a capaci-

tor in the system to allow for reliable starting if the battery was flat. Norton predominantly used Lucas equipment throughout the life of the model. The alternator was a six-pole laminated iron stator bolted to the inner primary chain case, energized by a six-pole permanent magnet stator bolted to the crankshaft, and initially rated at 120 watts. The AC current from the alternator was converted to DC by a Lucas plate type rectifier and a Zener diode was used to regulate the current by 'dumping' excess voltage to earth. The system gave a reliable and robust electrical system that enabled the use of reasonably powerful headlights and put to bed many of the Lucas 'Prince of Darkness' myths that still surround British electrics. The rectifier was mounted on the frame's back bracing plate and the Zener was initially fixed to a circular alloy heat sink mounted behind the front of the drive-side panel. The Zener was relocated to the 'Z' plate in 1969 with the 'S' type.

The pre-1971 Commandos had a small pressed tin switch on the left-hand bar, pressed steel levers and small numbers on the speedo and tachometer.

The Commando from 1971 had Lucas handlebar switches, a chromed headlamp with three warning lights and the lights toggle switch.

The initial Commando headlamp was a 7in Lucas unit, which in 1968 housed a main beam warning light, toggle light switch and an ammeter. A 40/50 watt dip main headlamp was fitted, giving state of the art lighting for the time. The ignition switch was a two position unit (power off or on), operated by a key, and the lights were controlled by the three-position toggle switch giving off/parking/main positions. Rider controls comprised a pressed steel circular switch cluster on the left-hand handlebar, with a main/dip toggle switch, and push-button horn and headlamp flasher. The brake light was operated from a micro switch mounted on the rear brake pedal bracket.

The electrical system was made more sophisticated for 1971. As it was pretty reliable, the ammeter was replaced by a red ignition warning light in the headlamp, which came on if the battery voltage dropped too low. The headlamp also carried a two-position toggle switch for the lights and indicator and main beam warning lights; the specifications show a 45/40 watt headlamp bulb. The ignition switch was located under the rider's left leg and was bolted onto an extension from the battery tray, with the lock facing forwards. This was a four-position switch, with two positions where the key could be removed (positions 1 and 2) and two where the key could not be removed (positions 3 and 4). Position 1 gave the parking (side) lights only and everything else off, position 2 was everything off, position 3 was ignition only and position 4 was ignition and lights. The side lights or main headlamp were selected using the switch on the headlamp when the ignition switch was in position 4. The direction indicators were optional, and when fitted were housed on chromed stems and a pressure-sensitive brake light switch was incorporated in the front brake cable, supplementing the rear brake switch.

The 1971 handlebar switches were new alloy units that incorporated the lever pivots and had nice forged alloy levers. The left and right hand looked the same, with a central toggle switch and a push button above and below it. The left-hand side unit used the push buttons for the horn and headlamp flasher, with a two-position toggle for dip and main, while the right-hand unit used one of its push buttons as an engine kill button, and the second push button was not used. The unit had a three-position toggle switch for the indicators, down for right and up for left. The units were a great advance on the cheap pressed steel units fitted previously but were not as good ergonomically as the latest Japanese offerings and were also unmarked as to their functions. The press was not too impressed, but in use they were reliable and, once the rider got used to them, were considered to be adequate.

The lever pivots were redesigned to lessen hand span and were painted black for 1972, and extended toggle switch blades were fitted for the 1973 model year. When the hydraulic disc brake was introduced in 1972, a hydraulic switch was incorporated into the master cylinder to operate the brake light. A halogen headlight was an option from 1973.

While the Commando generally was equipped with a Lucas 7in chromed headlamp, the 'SS' type and the Hi-Rider were equipped with a 5¾in (14.6cm) diameter headlamp, but retained the three warning lights and light switch. The headlamp was retained by chromed brackets mounted between the yokes, apart from on the 'S' and 1970 Roadsters, when a chromed tubular loop was used.

This electrical system remained broadly unchanged until the introduction of the Mark 3. The John Player Norton, however, came with a 180 watt alternator with twin Zener diode regulation to allow for the extra power needed for the twin 40/45 watt headlamps fitted to the JPN style fairing.

The John Player Norton charging system and high power alternator were carried over to the Mark 3, along with a number of other improvements. The headline addition to the Mark 3 electrical system was the electric start, which was an American 'Prestolite' unit bolted to the top of the primary chain case and driving the crankshaft through a train of gears. The starter required a solenoid and high capacity cable connecting the battery directly to the motor.

A beefed-up battery was fitted to try to cope with the electric starter, which was kept charged by the 180 watt alternator. Other electrical

During 1972 the lever pivots were changed and painted black, and from 1973 extended toggle switch blades were fitted.

The Mark 3 had up-to-date switches that rivalled the Japanese offerings, and the warning lights and ignition switch grouped in a neat and visible console.

Neat Commando Features

The Commando shows a lot of interesting thinking and some quite clever production engineering solutions, indicating that Norton obviously put a lot of thought into reusing items and making one thing do two jobs.

Both of the footrests carrying 'Z' plates are virtually identical – same casting, same machining and same studs and bolts – apart from the timing side one having an extra hole to carry the Zener diode. This meant that Norton could gain a lower price for the raw casting as it could be ordered in volume for production. Of course the 'Z' plates were a defining element of the Commando's styling and were quite unlike anything seen previously, as well as providing a sturdy and simple fixing for the exhausts and footrests.

The early model Commandos mounted their Zener diode on a separate heat sink mounted behind the side panel on the drive side, where cooling could be marginal. On later models, the timing side 'Z' plate carried the Zener diode and acted as a heat sink. It was ideal for the purpose as it was made of alloy (a good heat conductor) and was out in the breeze, meaning that the separate heat sink and its mounting bracket were no longer required. Twin Zeners were fitted on the Mark 3s with their three-phase alternator, one on each 'Z' plate.

The rear brake lever was retained on its shaft by a special extended grease nipple. The nipple fitted into a groove in the shaft, so the lever could not fall off and the grease that travelled down the extension was delivered to where it was needed. Again making one item do two jobs, it was a simple and elegant solution.

The rectifier was bolted to the back plate of the frame just behind the end of the main spine, and its bolt was used as a second fixing to locate the top side panel retaining bracket. Rather than drill an extra hole in the frame to mount the rectifier and have an extra bolt to locate the bracket, the rectifier does both jobs.

The sludge trap in the bolt up crank was formed from the hollow big end journals. This gave a large capacity for sludge and was relatively easy to get at to clean (unlike Triumph and BSA's tube within the journals, located by a flywheel bolt and accessed through a plug that was always impossible to remove). The Commando sludge trap's large volume, however, meant that it was vital to prime the system before starting after a rebuild to get oil to the big ends, which takes a considerable amount of oil.

The knurled nuts used to fix the seat in place were a simple and easy way of making the seat quickly detachable without the rider needing any tools. Maintenance-free and utilizing the top mounts of the rear shock absorbers, they were user friendly, simple, used few parts and again added a neat styling touch to the bike.

The frame is a paragon of simplicity. As it did not need to damp out vibration it could be made much lighter than previous Featherbeds, saving about 11lb (5kg), and its large diameter spine gave it great rigidity. There is a minimum of extra bracketry added to support ancillaries and apart from the steering head there are no bearings. Even the steering lock simply butts against a lug on the headstock, with no complex brackets with holes for the lock to engage with.

Norton made extensive use of standard-sized spacers to enable the use of simple brackets. A case in point is the fixing for the rear mudguard bracket. The bracket is a simple square-shaped steel plate with three holes and a bend across its centre, and must have been simple and easy to fabricate. It is held onto the frame by two bolts and spacers (part number 062170), which are the same as that used to mount the top of the air filter box to the frame.

The 'S' type and first year of the Roadster had a chromed steel ring mount for the headlamp.

The Mark 3's electric start was positioned at the back of the motor and drove the crank through the primary chain case.

improvements were a neat warning light and ignition switch console placed between the instruments, at long last putting the ignition switch in a sensible position.

The Mark 3 was equipped with redesigned black-painted handlebar switches, which were much more ergonomic and had the switch function cast in the housing and picked out in white. The warning lights (including a neutral indicator) were repositioned in a semicircular console bolted onto the top yoke between the speedo and tachometer.

The main beam, charging (ignition) and indicator warning lights were joined by a neutral light, connected to a switch on the front of the gearbox and operated from an indent in the surface of the gear change camplate. The ignition switch was the same four-position unit fitted to the post-1970 models. The handlebar switches were all new, satin black units with much better ergonomics than the previous units. The right-hand unit had an up and down sliding switch to select pilot or main lights, a side to side off-on-off kill switch and the all important electric start button on the lower front of the unit in green. The left-hand cluster mirrored the design of the right unit with an up and down dip and main, side to side indicators and a combined horn and headlamp flasher push button (in for horn and up for headlamp flasher) at the lower front. The switch functions were cast into the housings and picked out in white. High quality forged and polished alloy levers were retained.

Instruments

The Commando had its two main instruments, the speedometer and tachometer, rigidly bolted into alloy cups that in turn bolted onto the top of the fork yoke using the fork stanchion nuts. This method of mounting the instruments with no rubber to isolate the delicate instruments from a twin's vibration was only viable because of the Commando's Isolastic system.

The cups were initially polished alloy finish but from the 1973 model year they were painted black and were extended in depth as deeper Italian Veglia instruments started to supplement and eventually replace the Smiths units. A special extension bolt was produced to allow the Smiths instruments to be bolted into the deeper cups. The 1974 model year saw a black plastic cover on the bottom of the cups. The Commando initially used Smiths instruments, and the speedometer did not have a trip mileage function. The instruments had the green globe logo on their faces and relatively fine print for the 0–150mph scale in 10mph increments and the 0–9,000rpm tachometer, making them relatively hard to read at speed. The face design of both instruments was improved for the 1971 model year when a larger font was used for the numbers. The green globe logo was retained, and the speedometer scale was redesigned with the numbering starting at 10mph and increasing in 20mph steps, making the face much clearer.

For the 1973 model year a trip function was provided on the Interstate's Veglia speedometer, and a white 'Norton' script was printed just below the centre of the dial as well as the green globe symbol on both of the Veglia instruments. By 1975 and the advent of the Mark 3 the instruments displayed the Norton Villiers Triumph 'Wiggly Worm' logo rather than the 'Norton' script. The Mark 3 parts book shows that Smiths instruments were fitted to the Roadster and Veglia instruments to the Interstate, and the illustration of the Roadster's Smiths speedometer does not have a trip. However, the Mark 3 UK and US brochures clearly show a trip-equipped Smiths speedometer. So it looks like any combination of Smiths and Veglia instruments were fitted at the factory.

Summary

The Commando was steadily developed during its lifetime and owners of earlier models can benefit from the myriad of improvements made throughout the models' life. However, what is significant is that the major components of the bike – the engine, frame and gearbox – did not change significantly throughout the life of the model range, indicating that the initial design team certainly got it right. There were some glitches (the Combat engine springs to mind) but the fundamentals of the model proved themselves capable for living for some ten years of production, which is pretty good for a bike with such a rushed initial design.

The original Commando had Smiths instruments, which featured the green blob branding mark.

Some of the later Veglia clocks carried the Norton Script logo. As they are deeper than the Smiths units, they are fitted in extended cups.

4 Competition History

Norton had a long and illustrious history in racing, starting from the first Isle of Man TT race in 1907, when Harold Rembrandt Fowler rode his own 690cc Peugeot V-twin powered Norton to victory in the twins class. Norton went on to dominate the racing scene throughout the first half of the twentieth century, latterly with their single and twin overhead camshaft single-cylinder Manx models, but by the end of the 1950s the Manx was starting to struggle against the multi-cylinder opposition. The early 1950s saw the emergence of the Dominator twin 500cc overhead valve engine in road racing with semi-official factory support, and Norton ran the Domiracer (as the racing twin was unofficially known) in the 1961 Isle of Man TT: ridden by Australian Tom Phillis it came a creditable third, behind two Manxes. This was really Norton's factory-backed racing swansong, however, and the race shop was closed in 1962 when the Bracebridge Street site was closed and Norton moved from Birmingham to the parent AMC site at Woolwich in London. The contents of the race shop, along with the Domiracer project, were sold off to Manchester dealer Reg Dearden and Paul Dunstall, the Eltham (south London) based tuner and racer, of whom more will be heard later.

The Norton race shop was housed in this building (or shed), which was still in existence at Andover circuit in 2010.

Norman White is No. 2, riding the 1974 F750 space frame Norton during the 1974 Thruxton 400 miler for GP bikes. No. 4 is Percy Tait on the works Triumph Trident and Kork Ballington is No.3 on the Kawasaki.

When the Commando was introduced, its potential for racing was recognized by the factory and customers were offered tuning kits developed by Paul Dunstall, who had lots of expertise racing the Norton twins. These kits gave rise to Norton offering its customers a factory-built production racer in autumn 1969. A picture of a drum-braked version appeared in the 1970 brochure. Cycle World carried out a test, again of a drum-braked version, in December 1969. For 1971 the Production Racer was a fully fledged offering from the renamed Norvil race shop, featuring the trademark yellow paint and a Lockheed front disc brake, and continued to be listed in the brochure until 1973.

In the meantime, the factory had been looking at the new F750 formula and Peter Williams designed a Commando-based F750 racer on a limited budget, using the Isolastic system, and he competed on it in 1971. The bike showed promise and towards the end of the year a major sponsorship deal was agreed with John Player and Sons, the cigarette manufacturer. The John Player Norton racing team was born.

The original F750 bike was redesigned for the 1972 season with a new tubular frame, retaining the Isolastics, and was painted in Ford Electric Blue, the Players No. 6 house colour. For 1973 the bikes sported a new monocoque chassis and numerous improvements, and a patriotic red, white and blue colour scheme. There was another new chassis for 1974, this time a tubular space frame, which was lighter and easier to repair than the monocoque. The John Player sponsorship was withdrawn at the end of 1974, and the team then concentrated on developing the new Cosworth-engined Challenge ready to race. The Challenge eventually made its racing debut at Brands Hatch in October 1975, but proved to be too little to late.

The final area that the Norton Commando excelled in was in sidecar motocross racing. The Commando engine was adopted by Wasp, a UK company run by Robin Rhind-Tutt, who was a successful racer in his own right. Wasp started to

The 1972 F750 was sponsored by John Player. Here the 1972 bike is undergoing a rebuild at Norman White's shop. Note the pannier fuel tanks and tubular frame.

produce Norton-powered outfits using the new Commando engine and gearboxes from 1969 and these dominated the European race scene until the mid-1970s. The engines were eventually bored out to 920cc, but these units tended to overstress the gearbox, leading to failure. The racers turned to overbored Yamaha XS650 units, which could be reliably overbored to 1000cc with a corresponding increase in power, outclassing the old Norton unit.

Formula 750 and the John Player Norton Team

With the Commando showing promise in production racing, in 1971 Peter Williams designed a Commando-based machine to compete in the new Federation International Motorsport (FIM) Formula 750cc (F750) open class. Using a tuned version of the Combat engine, the bike had a new frame that still followed the layout of the Commando, featuring Isolastic engine and gearbox mountings, twin down tubes, a single large diameter top tube and the characteristic forward sloping tubes running from the swing arm to the top tube. The spoked wheels featured alloy rims with a Manx-style conical rear hub and AP Lockheed front disc brake, while the low profile fuel tank and

central rubber-mounted oil tank were also fabricated in light alloy. The twin exhaust pipes swept under the centre of the crankcases and both exited on the right-hand side into stubby megaphones to maximize ground clearance. A custom-made single seat and a half fairing modified from the Production Racer finished off the plot. Initially the project had support and sponsorship from Hepolite, AP Lockheed, Champion spark plugs and Castrol, and the bike showed significant promise. Denis Poore recognized the bike's potential and set about looking for a significant sponsor to finance the race effort, and came up with a sponsorship deal with John Player and Sons, creating the John Player Norton team. Set up in late 1971, the team competed in the most popular production racer classes of the day, the FIM Formula 750 class and the American Motorcycle Association (AMA) rule book chapter XIII C: and E: classes.

The JPS team was managed by Frank Perris and had Peter Williams as the development engineer and chief rider, and Phil Read and Tony Rutter as the other riders. Williams continued to develop the bike and had the engines producing just less than 70bhp. He introduced innovations such as a MIRA wind tunnel-developed fairing that was designed to enable the rider to tuck in

The 1972 F750 was innovative from the start with its aerodynamic bodywork and sophisticated tubular frame. This bike was pictured at the National Motorcycle Museum in early 2010.

and minimize wind resistance, pannier fuel tanks to keep the centre of gravity low and decrease the frontal area, and placed the oil cooler in the seat tail to reduce wind resistance. All the bikes were equipped with Quaife five-speed gearboxes and were finished in a light blue (Ford Electric Blue) to match the colours of Player's No. 6 cigarette packets. Even in these early days innovation was the name of the game to make up for the relative lack of engine power from the Norton unit. The bikes were equipped with a cush drive in the back wheel; the bike pictured has a Manx hub, reversed with a bolt-on cush drive and the brake drum placed on the other side. The modified cush drive did not help with the gearbox failures that dogged the 1972 season: the gearbox mainshaft was flexing, causing the gears to separate and lose teeth and break. The cush drives were made up during the 1972 TT races to try to fix the problem, but both bikes suffered gearbox failure. The solution was a mainshaft outrigger system designed by Peter Williams and developed by the race shop. This had a new inner primary case with a set of needle roller bearings to support the mainshaft outboard of the final drive sprocket and inboard of the clutch, and the clutch ran dry. The oil cooler was originally fitted in the seat

An electronic tachometer is the only instrumentation on the 1972 F750. The two filler caps are both for fuel, the larger for the pannier tanks, the smaller for the fuel header tank.

The bike was equipped with a mechanical fuel pump, driven off the swinging arm. This transferred the fuel from the low pannier tanks to the header tank, which fed the carbs.

The tail originally housed the oil cooler, which was a Chevrolet automatic transmission cooler, and was fitted at Daytona.

hump, but was moved to the front of the bike during the season. The cooler was a Chevrolet automatic transmission cooler, originally fitted during the race week at Daytona. The front forks were based on standard Roadholders, but had shortened stanchions and much modification to the damping rates. The bike was fitted with pannier fuel tanks, with a fuel pump feeding a header tank driven from the swinging arm. As the suspension went up and down this operated the lever on the tank: the Suzuki team saw the Norton riders bouncing up and down on the grid to keep the header tank topped up and thought that they were warming up the suspension – so copied them …

The team's first big event was the US Daytona race of February 1972, in which the team rider Phil Read made a great start to the season and came in fourth place behind three Yamaha TZ350 two strokes, beating the BSA/Triumph triples. Peter Williams was not so lucky and did not finish due to gearbox failure. Read repeated the feat in March with a fourth place at the Imola 200 miler. Rutter left the team and was replaced with the up-and-coming Mick Grant.

June saw a bad F750 TT on the Isle of Man as the JPN bikes all failed to finish due to mechanical problems. The JPN team finally came good when Mick Grant won the Gold Cup meeting at Olivers Mount and Read took first place at the Hutchinson 100 at Brands Hatch, with Williams coming third.

Despite the aging engines, the fine handling and technological innovations were coming up trumps for the team. Norman White described riding the F750 bikes as:

> … like running on a monorail, not just running on rails. The bikes steered superbly, were very stable and did not need a steering damper even on the notoriously bumpy Gerard's Bend on the Mallory Park circuit.

The only downside that Norman White could think of was that they were a bit slow in changing direction through chicanes, where the bike has to flick from left to right to left (or vice versa) in quick succession.

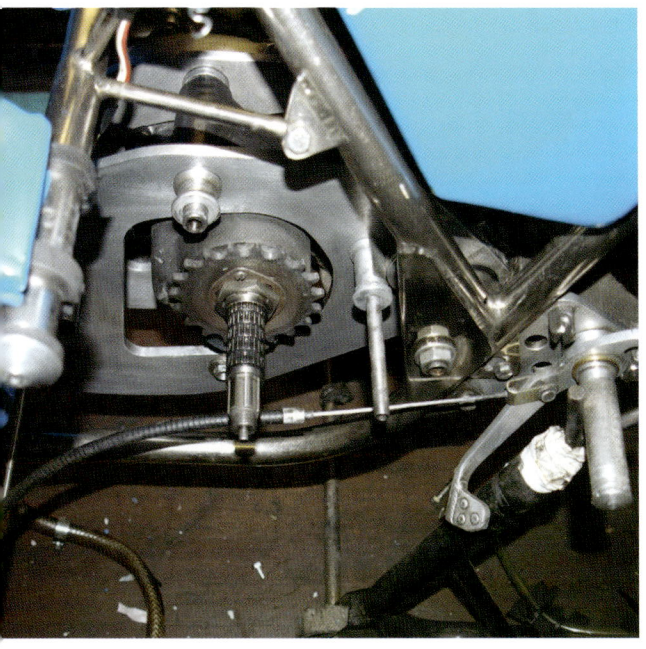

The F750 bikes suffered gearbox failures until an outrigger bearing was fitted between the gearbox sprocket and the clutch. Here are the roller bearings on the gearbox mainshaft.

The chain case was modified to carry the outrigger bearing. This supported the mainshaft and stopped it flexing, preserving the gearbox. Norman White holds the chain case from the 1973 monocoque racer, with belt drive.

The 1973 season saw a patriotic colour change to the red, white and blue of the John Player No. 10 brand, and technological innovations continued with the introduction of the famous monocoque frame. The prototype was made using mild steel, but the four racers' frames were produced in stainless steel. The unit was double-skinned to carry the fuel and oil, but the original plan to carry oil in the rear of the unit had to be abandoned due to overheating, and the oil was carried in a separate tank ahead of the engine. The new chassis weighed some 37lb (16.75kg) and gave a significant weight saving over the previous year's tubular frame.

Five monocoque chassis were made, but only four complete bikes were assembled. All four bikes survive in various states of originality. Dave Croxford's bike was crashed by him at the Silverstone International and effectively destroyed (the damaged monocoque was presented to Croxford as a standard lamp, engraved with the text 'five weeks to build and five seconds to break') but it

has been completely restored and is now back in one piece.

The monocoque bikes scored many successes during 1974, including Peter Williams and Mick Grant coming first and second in the F750 Isle of Mann TT race, first places in the Anglo American Race series at both Mallory Park and Oulton Park, and other firsts at the Cadwell Park and Scarborough MCN Superbike races, and at Brands Hatch.

Gulf Oil provided additional sponsorship for 1974, which saw the advent of a new tubular frame for the racer, which was lighter and easier to repair than the monocoque, but not as innovative.

The Commando engine was showing its age, however, and competition from Japan was hotting up with the purpose-built big multi-cylinder two-stroke engined bikes, such as the Yamaha TZ750 and TZ350, producing much more power than the now dated production-based Commando unit.

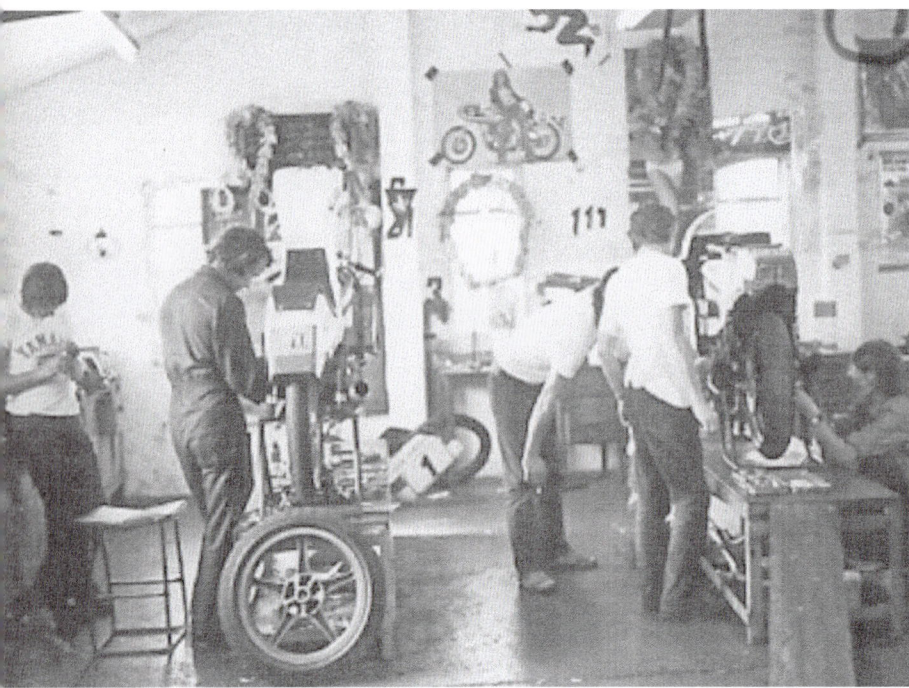

View of the Norton race shop in 1973. There are two monocoques visible. (Left to right) Tony Wood, Robin Clyst, Basil Knight (bent over) and Mike Eber-Davis.

The 1973 monocoque F750 reverted to red, white and blue John Player colours. Double disc front brakes and aerodynamic fairings over the rider's hands helped the bike to stop and go.

Norman White demonstrates the lightweight bodywork on the 1973 Monocoque. The seat/tank unit hinged upwards to give access to the top of the bike.

With the tank/seat unit hinged up out of the way, the top of the monocoque is exposed. Norman's hand is indicating where cold air was ducted across the top of the head.

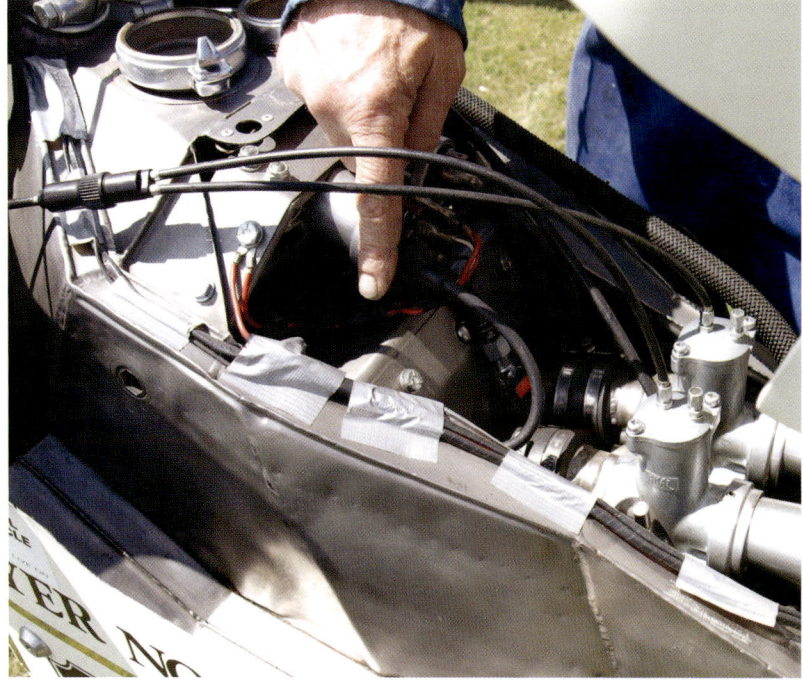

The new frames were a last attempt to reduce the bike's weight and frontal area to try to offset its power deficiency. While the Nortons' performance was improved, the massive power differential between them and the opposition could not be bridged by their superb handling and road holding and the Nortons were simply overwhelmed.

That year Peter Williams had a disastrous crash at Oulton Park. A picture that appeared in the press gave rise to a myth that this crash was caused by the seat/tank unit of his bike becoming detached, throwing him and the bike onto the track. Norman White pointed out to the author that, while the loss of the seat was reported at the time to have caused the crash, in fact it was not the cause. By the time the photograph was taken the bike had already crashed, and the seat tank unit was coming off because of the crash. The injuries Williams sustained, while not fatal, ended his racing career.

By then, recognizing that the Commando unit was nearing the end of its competition life, the factory was looking to replace the Commando

Close-up of the front of the 1973 monocoque showing the oil tank and filler.

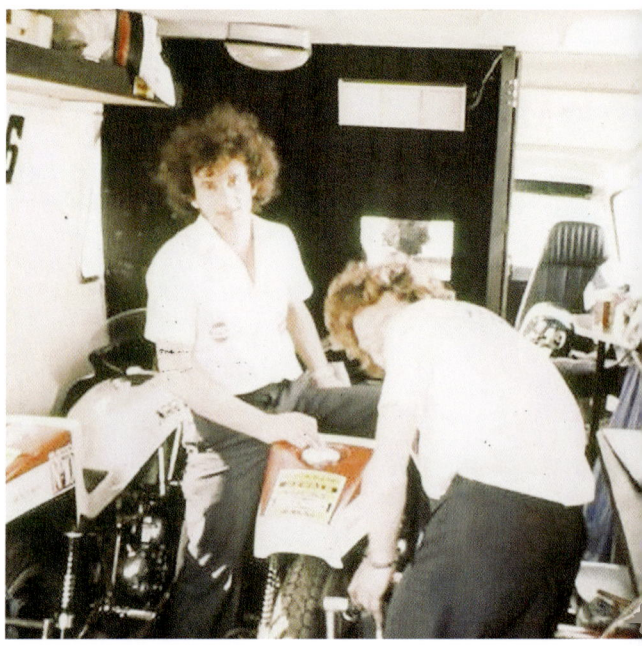

View of the race shop personnel with the famous John Player Team van (left to right): chief engine man Dave Ludwell, machinist John Fox, engine man Reg Painter, Norman White on the bike, mechanic/frame builder Peter Pyket, draughtsman Basil Knight, welder Robin Clyst, apprentice Mike Ember-Davis, mechanic Tony Wood, administrator Ernest Harper.

View inside the Norton race team van at Spa Francorchamps, Belgium, 1974. Note the space frames. Here are Norman White and John McClaren, while Peter Williams is visible in the front cabin.

Norman White on the 1974 F750 space frame, with his rear wheel off the ground during the 400 miler Thruxton for GP bikes. The crank broke on the second lap and the alternator rotor broke off. The bike carried on but the damage eventually took out the whole crank.

Peter Williams on F750 Space Frame no. 22 during 1974.

The 1974 F750 Space Frame was now also sponsored by Gulf Oil and featured cast alloy wheels.

Pictured at Norman White's premises at Thruxton are a works Production Racer,
1973 monocoque and the Norton Cosworth Challenge.

engine with the Cosworth Challenge, a water-cooled eight-valve twin that was based on two cylinders of the Cosworth V8 Formula 1 grand prix engine, but it was all too late. The factory withdrew from racing at the end of the season, and the Commando's days as a works racer ended.

Production Racing

At the introduction of the Commando in 1968, Norton offered conversion kits that gave customers the choice of three levels of tune. The kits were developed in collaboration with Paul Dunstall, who had a great deal of experience in tuning Norton twins. Dunstall had been racing a Norton twin in the 1950s and then sponsored riders while he concentrated on the tuning. He bought the contents of Norton's race shop

when it closed in 1962, acquiring the works 'Domiracer' and Norton's tuning knowhow. This helped to expand his offerings to the general public and enabled him to offer tuning goodies and complete machines to the public all through the 1960s and early 1970s. His Norton Dominator-based bikes were offered as fast road-legal café racers and as pure racers, and had a great reputation, to the extent that Dunstall was recognized as a bike manufacturer in his own right. Probably the high spot in Dunstall's early career was when one of his Dominator-based racers won the 1968 production Isle of Man TT. With this background it was pretty much inevitable that Norton would turn to him to provide the tuning kits.

The Stage 1 kit gave a claimed 10 per cent power increase with no loss of flexibility. The kit comprised:

The Commando Production Racer was first seen in 1969 and featured the standard Commando chassis and a tuned motor. The picture shows Norman White riding in the 1973 Thruxton 500 miler, which he won with Rex Butcher as co-rider. The bike had already won the 1970 and 1972 Thruxton 500 milers.

- 1 pair of 10:1 pistons
- 1 pair of special material exhaust valves
- 3 pairs of carb main jets
- 1 pair of racing spark plugs
- 1 pair of 'patent' silencers (Dunstall's own 'deci-bel' design)
- Top end overhaul gasket set
- Timing disc
- 1 pair of tank decals

The Stage 2 kit gave a 16 per cent power boost, and improved acceleration in the middle ranges of rpm. It comprised:
- 1 pair of 10:1 pistons
- 1 pair of special material exhaust valves
- 1 pair of new inlet valves with a different collet position
- 1 set of 'special' valve springs
- 1 pair of induction manifolds

- 3 pairs of carb main jets
- 1 pair of racing spark plugs
- New special camshaft
- 1 pair of tuned length and diameter exhaust pipes
- 1 pair of 'patent' silencers (Dunstall's own 'deci-bel' design)
- Complete gasket set
- Timing disc
- 1 pair of tank decals

The Stage 3 kit gave a 20 per cent power boost, and converted the bike to full production racing specification. It comprised:
- 1 pair of 10:1 pistons
- 1 pair of special material exhaust valves
- 1 pair of new inlet valves with different collet position
- 1 set of 'special' valve springs

Dunstall Conversion Kits

	Standard	Stage 1	Stage 2	Stage 3
Power increase	–	10%	16%	20%
Top speed (mph)	114	120	130	137
Max speed in gears (mph):				
3rd	90	92	108	110
2nd	65	67	78	80
1st	42	43	51	53
Acceleration (secs):				
0–60mph	4.75	4.6	4.4	4.1
0–80mph	9.0	8.25	7.5	6.9
0–100mph	15.0	13.75	12.75	11.5

- 1 pair of flexible induction manifolds
- 1 pair of 1½in bore Amal Concentric carburettors
- 1 pair of racing spark plugs
- Domiracer camshaft
- 1 set of special cam followers
- 1 pair of racing exhaust pipes
- 1 pair of racing megaphones
- Complete gasket set
- Timing disc
- 1 pair of tank decals

Along with the three conversion kits, Norton also offered a customizing kit. This was aimed at the fast road rider or racer rather than an early 'Hi-Rider' conversion, and provided all the modifications to the running rear needed to create a racing machine. Again it was based on Paul Dunstall's expertise in providing café racers for the road and real racers, and the kit comprised:
- Clip-on handlebars
- Headlamp brackets
- Alloy, ball-ended brake and clutch levers with built-in 'star' adjusters
- Alloy 19in diameter front and rear wheel rims
- 19in rear wheel spokes
- 19in Avon Grand Prix rear tyre, tube and rim tape
- Alloy top fork yoke
- Front fork rubber gaiters
- Rear shock absorber rubber gaiters
- Rear-mounted footrests
- Transfers for the rider's helmet

The combination of the various tuning kits and the customization kit meant that Norton's customers had the option to produce a bike that met their individual requirements. Since the kits were offered by Norton, it also meant that Norton gained the revenue for the parts, rather than seeing the custom going to third-party tuners, as had happened in the past.

For 1970 Norton started to produce batches of production racers, based on the tuning kits but using different bodywork. While pictures of these appeared in the 1970 brochure, they do not seem to have been actively marketed until 1971, when the 750cc FIM (Fédération Internationale Motorsport) approved Production Class racer appeared. This bike sported the now famous 'Norvil' style tank and seat, with its built-in racing number plate, a half fairing and a disc front brake with Lockheed racing calliper. Norton also offered a transistorized ignition system and a five-speed gearbox as options on these bikes. The Production Racer continued to be offered in 1972, with a 'Norvil' front disc and a 'specially assembled high compression engine', which housed a Norvil 'Triple S' camshaft.

With the introduction of the 828cc engine (bore and stroke of 77 × 89mm) in 1973, the original 750cc (bore and stroke of 73 × 89mm) unit was replaced with a new short stroke version of the 828cc unit, with a bore and stroke of 77 × 80mm.

The works PRs had some subtle
modifications that were not passed
on to the customer machines. This
is a 1973 model in JPN colours.

Pegasus ran two supercharged
Commando engines: the plumbing
was impressive.

The Specialists: Paul Dunstall and Gus Kuhn

Two of the most famous tuners of Commandos in the late 1960s and early 1970s were Paul Dunstall and Gus Kuhn Motors. Paul Dunstall bought the contents of the Norton race shop in the early 1960s and specialized in tuning and developing the Featherbed-framed twins, including the Atlas, to the extent of being recognized as a manufacturer in his own right with the Dunstall Domiracer. Dunstall's expertise in engine tuning was used to produce his own range of engine tuning parts, including camshafts for road and racing, venier sprockets for fine tuning the camshaft timing, larger valves, high compression pistons and various lightened valve train components. With the introduction of the Commando, Dunstall continued to offer complete bikes based on the model, with tuned engines and all the racing accessories such as single or dual racing-style seats, alloy or glass fibre racing fuel tanks, rear sets, clip-ons, racing exhausts and fairings. His patented Dunstall 'Decibel' exhausts were probably the best-known (and surprisingly one of the quieter) aftermarket 'silencers' for the British Café Racer of the early 1970s with its clean shape and trademark seven circular outlets within the end cone. He also offered a bolt-on 810cc conversion for the 750cc, which comprised a new alloy barrel that was half the weight of the standard iron unit, new pistons, rings and crankcase and barrel studs. Dunstall claimed the kit gave 70bhp at 7,000rpm, a substantial increase over the standard 750. Dunstall also offered all of his range of parts separately so that owners could customize their bikes, and was notable for offering twin hydraulically operated disc brakes with the callipers integrally cast with the fork sliders. Dunstall's ultimate offering was a spine-framed racer, powered by a Commando engine.

Paul Dunstall and Gus Kuhn produced catalogues and tuning guides to help promote their Norton expertise.

Gus Kuhn Motors was a London-based Norton dealer who started a race team in 1968 under the auspices of Vincent Davey, the son-in-law of the company founder Gus Kuhn. The 1969 race effort comprised two 350cc and two 500cc Seeleys and a couple of Commando Production Racers. The team put a Commando engine into one of the Seeley frames to create a 'proper' racer for unlimited races, and also used the PR bikes in the unlimited class. While the Seeley-framed bikes discarded the Isolastics, the engines were mildly tuned and used parts were readily available from Norton. During 1973 the team even campaigned a bike equipped with the Dunstall 810cc conversion in 1000cc events. The secret of their success was in the meticulous preparation and build of the engines. Part of the effort also produced Commando-based specials, both in Production Racer trim for road use and to short circuit racing specification. Like Dunstall, as well as producing complete bikes Kuhn also supplied racing parts for the Commando owner, with a range remarkably similar to Dunstall's, including race-developed exhausts, clip-ons, rear sets, seats, tanks and fairings. The range was less extensive than Dunstall's and the tuning operation followed Norton's own doctrine, using Norton parts rather than developing their own engine components, but the Kuhn Commandos had a good reputation for performance and reliability. Both Dunstall and Kuhn bikes are still sought after today and are recognized as 'legitimate' classics in their own right.

Drag Racing: Pegasus and Hogslayer

The Commando engine's combination of power and torque made it a natural for drag racing. With the standard 750 turning in standing-start quarter-mile times in the low 13 seconds, and the 850 matching these times, the Commando was taken up by the drag racing fraternity on both sides of the Atlantic.

This frontal view of Pegasus shows very 1970s airbrushed art and a slim profile.

Around the mid-1970s the quest for power in two-wheeled drag racing led to the appearance of twin-engined dragsters, for which the Norton, with its separate engine and gearbox, was a natural choice. Two of the most famous drag bikes of the era were the UK's Pegasus and the US's Hogslayer.

Pegasus was the brainchild of Derek Chinn and Ian Messenger, and comprised two supercharged 850 Norton units, comprising 750cc crankcases opened out to take 850 barrels (giving 1656cc), running 7:1 compression ratio pistons, steel Carrillo con rods and initially a standard SS camshaft, with pair of Shorrocks 75B super-

chargers, one for each unit. At first it featured an AMC gearbox, using just third and top gear, and eventually switched to a purpose-built two-speed Lenco unit. The bike was taken on by *Bike* magazine, which offered some sponsorship and featured it as its 'Project Bike' through the 1970s. Pegasus was successfully raced until 1979. Its best result was 8.4 seconds for a quarter mile, with a terminal speed of 170mph.

Hogslayer was built by T. C. Christenson, a US Norton dealer, and came in three incarnations. The final twin-engined version had a Hilbourn fuel injection system, slider clutch, two-speed gearbox adapted from a Rambler car overdrive

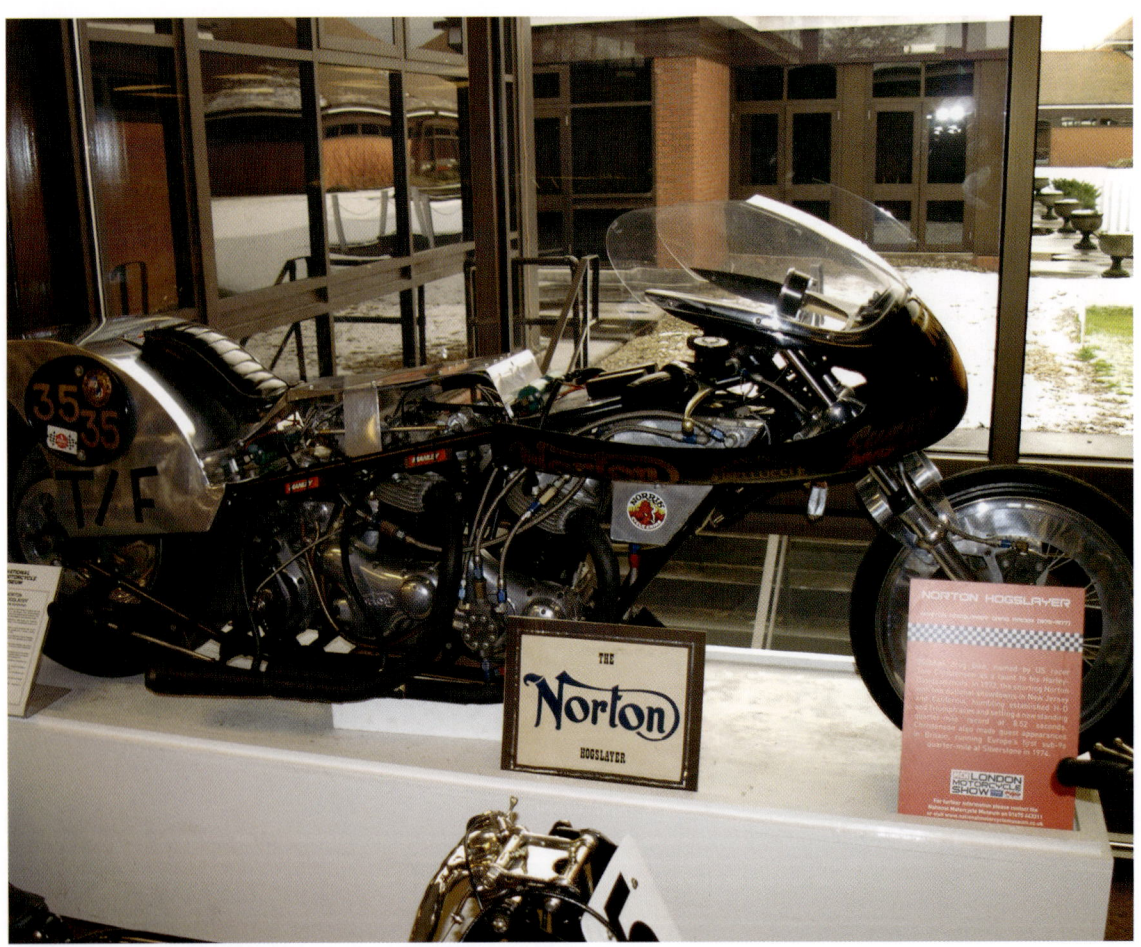

Hogslayer was named after its ability to beat Hogs (Harley-Davidsons) at the track.
One of its innovations was the extremely wide rear tyre.

In contrast to Pegasus, Hogslayer
was normally aspirated, but was
equipped with Hilbourn fuel
injection.

The ill-fated Norton Triumph
American Racing Team from the
1975 US brochure.

unit and, burning nitro-methane, produced some 300bhp. The bike ran mid-7 second quarter miles with an elapsed speed of 180mph. Christenson won the National Hot Rod Association US Nationals in 1972 and the NHRA Top Fuel series in 1973.

US Short Track and TT Racing

The Commando engine did not make much of a mark in US flat track racing. Norton sponsored a team the Norton Triumph American Racing Team, that ran three bikes in the AMA Grand National series in 1975, but the effort folded when the factory went down, with few results.

The scene was dominated by Triumph and Harley-Davidson twins until Ron Wood, the owner of a lampshade factory, who had been riding since 1947, stepped up to the mark. In 1967 he was watching a half-mile racing with some friends and made the mistake of telling them that he could build a bike that was better and faster

than those competing. One of his friends said, 'You make it, I'll ride it': so he did. While his first bike didn't win, it did show some promise. In 1971 Ron started to build his first Norton-based bike, although it took a year for him to iron out the problems and start winning.

Wood worked closely with C. R. Axtell, who ran a machine shop and dynometer, and by 1977 was getting a genuine 81bhp at the rear wheel, with plenty of torque. Two bikes were built, each with a different custom-built frame. The first of these used a 3in diameter 20 gauge chrome-molybdenum tube to form a loop that encircled the engine and gearbox. Oil was carried in the loop, and there was a neat curved cut-out on the front of the down tube to give the front wheel room to move. The second frame used two small diameter tubes to cradle the engine and to connect the steering head to a square section oil tank.

Both of the frames were painted bright red and carried a minimal 2gal fuel tank and seat. The engines were highly tuned, with polished and

Ron Wood's Norton-powered flat track racer went as well as it looked. Note the subtle shaving of the front down tube to allow for wheel clearance. This picture was taken by Peter Sakai at the 2007 Legends of the Motorcycle meeting in Half Moon Bay, near San Francisco.

The 2 gal fuel tank on the Ron Wood Norton was just enough to complete a typical race and looked superb. The bike here was photographed by Frank Charriaut, again at the 2007 Legends of the Motorcycle meeting in Half Moon Bay.

balanced internals, and used standard con rods. Carburation was by a pair of huge Dellortos mounted on long rubber inlet tracts and Axtell exhaust systems were fitted, with an individual pipe and silencer per cylinder. Riders included Alex Jorgenson and John Hateley, and the bikes dominated their home track, Ascot Park in Southern California, during the mid-1970s.

To back up the message there was a huge advertising billboard at the track with the slogan 'Lotta torque about Norton'– the defining characteristic of the Commando engine!

Pictured here by Frank Charriaut, the Ron Wood Norton used a large diameter tube to form the main frame, and was a very good-looking bike.

Cosworth – Norton's Challenge

With the Commando engine getting a bit long in the tooth and not giving enough reliable power for the JPN racers, Norton looked to the racing car engine manufacturer Cosworth Engineering for a replacement. Cosworth made the very successful DFV 3-litre V8 engine that was used by many Formula 1 race teams at the time. Norton wanted a twin, and Cosworth used the overall cylinder layout, combustion chamber design and cylinder dimensions of the DFV to come up with a 750cc twin with an 85.7 × 64.8mm bore and stroke, which featured four valves per cylinder, double overhead camshafts and water cooling.

Two engines were envisaged: type JAA was intended for a production road bike and had a compression ratio of 10.5:1, while JAB was intended for racing and had a compression ration of 11:1. The engine was an all alloy unit, with a toothed belt drive on the left-hand side of the 360-degree crank to an idler gear in the head that drove the two camshafts. The belt also drove a balancer shaft located behind the cylinder block, while a second balancer shaft was gear driven and located ahead of the crankshaft. Twin Amal Mark II carburettors were fitted, and the crankcase and gearbox were formed from a single alloy casing, with the wet iron cylinder liners spigotted into the upper half of the casting. The casting was horizontally split through the main bearings in typical automotive practice. The gearbox was a five-speed crossover design, with the clutch chain driven on the right and the output sprocket on the left. The engine

The Cosworth-engined Challenge was the replacement for the Commando-engined F750.

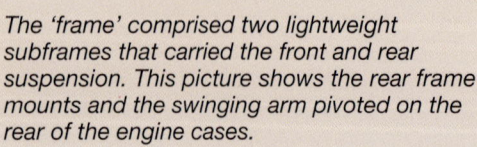

The 'frame' comprised two lightweight subframes that carried the front and rear suspension. This picture shows the rear frame mounts and the swinging arm pivoted on the rear of the engine cases.

was massively built and designed to be a stressed member of the frame, and had the swinging arm pivot incorporated in the rear of the gearbox. Power output of the racing engine was a claimed 95bhp at 9,750rpm.

The engine was fielded in the Norton Challenge racer in 1975, which had a number of unique features in keeping with the Norton race shop's record of innovation. The engine, as intended, formed part of the frame, with a tubular subframe attached to the top of the engine to support the steering head, an alloy swinging arm pivoted on the rear of the engine casing, and twin shocks attached to a second lightweight tubular subframe attached to the rear of the engine. Cast alloy wheels were used and the rear carried its disc brake outside of the swinging arm on the same side as the sprocket, a complicated system that gave a quickly detachable wheel for fast tyre changes.

Time was against the Challenge. Despite Norton's increasingly dubious financial state, the bike was raced at Brands Hatch towards the end of the 1975 season, but was taken out in a first corner crash on the first day, and then the engine failed after overheating the following day. The bike as a whole needed more development time and effort to improve reliability, increase the power and cut down the weight, but the emergence of the cheap, fast and reliable Suzuki RG500 and Yamaha TZ750 two-stroke racers meant the end of the four stroke in large capacity racing in the 1970s.

The Challenge continued the Norton F750 tradition of innovative design.

5 Owning and Riding

The Commando is probably one of the best-supported British classics, and it has a cadre of enthusiastic owners' clubs and dealers who are continually improving the product. I would recommend that any Commando owner invests in a copy of the Norton Owners Club Commando Service Notes and the International Norton Owners Association's INOA Tech Digest (for full details see the Bibliography below). Both are full of hints and tips on running and maintaining the bikes. Also, if an owner is contemplating working on his or her bike, a parts catalogue and workshop manual are a must. The workshop manual takes you through the dismantling and reassembly of most parts of the bike and the parts catalogue gives exploded diagrams of all the sub-assemblies, showing the order of assembly of units and all the part numbers.

This chapter examines the major areas of improvement open to current owners, and then looks at the experiences of past and present Commando owners and riders. Bear in mind that, while this chapter will provide details of problems and fixes, it does not mean that a Commando is unreliable! Many Commandos provided sterling service to their owners and most in use today provide their owners with a pleasurable riding experience, demonstrating that the model has the performance and stamina to carry out long-distance touring and fast scratching with equal aplomb. Some owners' experiences are given in the second part of the chapter and these show that there is much expertise and experience out there dedicated to improving the breed.

Commandos are often customized. This fine example sports lots of alloy, including fuel and oil tanks, neat seat, rear sets and non-standard carbs.

Improvements

Running Gear

First up with the running gear is to upgrade the Isolastics to the Mark 3 'vernier' adjustment type. This cuts out the fiddly and labour-intensive shimming needed to ensure the correct frame to mount clearances, and makes it a lot easier and convenient to carry out this vital maintenance task. Kits are available from most good Norton suppliers and should also include instructions on fitting and maintaining. Finally, if your Isolastics are old, then it is worth renewing the rubbers. As noted in Chapter 3, the rear swinging arm bushes must be lubricated with oil, not grease. It is well worthwhile cleaning out the wicks and drillings in the pivot pin from time to time, and re-oiling to avoid premature wear.

While it is unlikely that there are any early frames with the plate gusseting around the steering head, if your bike has one then you have a very rare beast that will probably break its frame around the top of the down tubes with potentially fatal results. So you have three choices: get the frame modified by welding in a bracing tube, change the frame for one with the lower bracing tube or don't ride the bike.

Some riders find that the standard footrests are too far forward and make for an uncomfortable riding position over distances. This is especially prevalent on the Interstate as the seat is a couple of inches further back, making the relative position of footrests worse. The quick fix for this is to fit rear-set footrests, and many kits are available.

The rear seat loop is not structural and is made out of relatively thin walled tubing. It is not designed to take a lot of weight, so don't fit a rack and only support it from this tube: make sure you have additional bracing down to the pillion footrests to take the weight. If you don't the loads from the rack will break or bend the rear loop of the frame.

Also carefully inspect any rack fitting that utilizes the top bolt of the rear suspension unit. The suspension unit pivots slightly around its top mount, and if it fouls the rack fittings then it may break the unit at the top mount.

Rear-set footrests are not just for Café Racers! As they move the position of the rider's feet back, they can help to make the riding position more comfortable for touring.

Ken Rawlinson's Mark 3 shows the correct way to fit a rack, with the struts from the rack to the pillion footrests to take the weight. Mounting the rack purely to the rear frame loop risks bending or breaking it.

Engine Improvements for Reliability

Careful assembly is probably the main action that owners can perform to improve engine reliability. Cleanliness of the workbench and components, liberal oiling of components and use of colloidal graphite on shell bearings and other moving parts all helps to prevent wear when an engine is first started up. An important point on the Commando is the size of the void in the crank pins, which is used as the sludge trap. This is a substantial volume that must be filled with oil before it makes its way to the big ends, so priming the crank before starting, by pumping oil into the cases via the rocker feed union on the timing case, is important.

A major improvement to the engine is to fit a full flow oil filter to the oil system. This was done by the factory from around 1973. A cartridge type oil filter kit (part number 064077) was listed by Norton as a retrofit for the Commando, and can be mounted on the rear of the gearbox cradle after drilling a pair of holes. The unit used a Citroen 2CV spin-on filter that screwed on to

a head unit, which in turn can be bolted to any flat surface. The head unit and replacement filters are widely available. Norton fitted it into the oil return line, where it can collect any debris created by the engine.

Superblend type main bearings are a must. These are well documented and give no problems in use: the likelihood is that most running Commandos have them fitted already. If the big ends need replacing and the crank needs regrinding, then it is vital to have the correct radius ground at the edges of the crank pin. This is specified in the official Norton workshop manual. If the radius is not correct then the stresses set up can result in a broken crankpin.

The 'Norton Smile' describes the state of the crankcases when they let go in a big way: the result is a semicircular crack that follows the line of the main bearing housing and looks as if the engine has a big grin. This problem is mainly a 750 issue and is usually the result of prolonged high revs with tuned engines – and tuned engines include Combats. Norton addressed the issue

This special 850 shows the sort of non-standard Commando that may be encountered.

with the later 750 cases and all 850 cases with a lot more metal around the main bearing housings. Some of the cause can be placed on the inadequate main bearings, since worn bearings impose more hammering loads on the cases, so Superblends also help. As a result make sure the main bearings of an earlier bike are in good condition and don't over-rev the engine.

The engine breather system on earlier 750 engines comprised a timed disc driven from the end of the camshaft, and is identified by the external vent on the front drive side of the engine, where an elbow takes a tube that is led back to the oil tank neck. This system generally worked well, but was relatively limited in the volume it could cope with and could be overwhelmed at high revs: the outlet piping has a small diameter of less than ½in (1 cm), whereas that of the contemporary 650 Triumph breather outlet was twice the diameter.

For 1972 the breather system was changed to a non-timed system with a tower bolted to the back of the crankcases, which again vented to the oil

The standard cartridge type oil filter as fitted on the rear of the gearbox cradle on Ken Rawlinson's Mark 3: an easy retro-fit with great benefits for engine life.

One of the ultimate engine modifications, carried out by Norvil, takes the capacity up to 1000cc.

The Norvil 1000cc conversion still looks remarkably standard.

tank neck and had much greater capacity and used a much larger pipe. This system could result in excessive oil being retained in the crankcases as the oil scavenge system on these engines was not as efficient as the earlier 750s or the 850s. The 850 saw the breather relocated to the top rear of the timing side crankcase half, where it performed satisfactorily. The later 750 can be modified by moving the breather outlet to the 850's location and drilling holes in the crankcase timing side to allow free passage of the gasses from the crankcases into the chest. Full details are given in the INOA Tech Digest (*see* Bibliography).

One final useful engine modification is the fitment of the Mark 3 timing case to earlier models. The cam chain is driven from the idler pinion, the outer end of which is supported by the timing cover. Norton recommended that the chain tension was set using an old case with a cutaway to access the tensioner, which is a bit of a waste of a timing case!

Up to 1972 the 750 had a timed breather driven from the camshaft. This was not ideal, as it could struggle with high revs and volumes.

The Mark 3 case has an inspection hole just behind the contact breaker points cover, which allows you to check the cam chain tension with the case in place.

Carburation

There are many options for the Norton owner who wants to improve the carburation, ranging from upgrading the original equipment to replacing the original equipment with improved instruments.

The standard Amal Concentric carburettor is a simple and relatively reliable instrument that gives a good compromise between cost, performance and fuel economy. The main problems that arise are wear and the hassle of balancing the pair of instruments. The wear issue is caused by the fit of the slide in the body. On the original design the body and slide are made from a soft alloy and both are subject to wear. This means a less than airtight fit and causes a weak and erratic mixture, leading to poor running. The cure is simple: fit new carburettors and use a brass or chromed slide, or have the carburettor body sleeved. This will solve the wear problem (unless you run without an air cleaner) and is relatively cheap to do. Properly set up, a pair of Concentrics will give excellent top end performance and perform well throughout the whole rev range. For those who do not want the hassle of adjusting and balancing a twin carburettor setup, single carburettor kits are available ranging from just the manifold to a complete kit comprising a carburettor, new manifold and all the cables needed. Fitting a single carburettor, however, does mean modifications to the air filter arrangements.

For owners who want to dump the Amal Concentrics there are two main options: fit Japanese Mikuni or Keihein instruments or, if you want to keep the bike British, Amal Concentric Mark 2s. Both of these carbs will need new inlet manifolds and information on jetting and set-up is available from the various suppliers. Their performance is as good as the Concentric Mark 1s, but they appear to be as prone to wearing out as quickly as a standard Mark 1. One disadvantage of the Mikuni is that it

Some owners like bigger tyres. Here a much larger modern tyre has been fitted, but a new swinging arm was required to give clearance.

This 750 has a Mark 3 timing case with the cam chain tension check port behind the points cover, and also sports a pair of Mikuni carburettors.

If twin Amals are too much hassle to set up, a single carburettor manifold can be bought to fit a single standard Concentric. Note the new air filter back plate with a single centralized hole that takes the standard rubber hose.

The SU carburettor is a Constant Velocity type and gives great fuel consumption. It's a tight fit in the Commando, but it can be done.

A single Mikuni carburettor is fitted to this very clean 850. Just visible is the clamp-on air filter that has replaced the standard unit.

appears to be available only in left-hand form, making them difficult to tune.

A final option is the fitting of a constant velocity SU carburettor. There was a conversion available in the 1970s and 1980s, and the 1976 Norton was equipped with a single 1¾in (40mm) SU, which was fitted mainly to improve the emissions of the bike but also improved fuel consumption by a claimed 40 per cent. The main problem with an SU conversion is the lack of clearance between the top of the carburettor and the main frame spine.

Primary Drive and Gearbox

The gearbox is considered by many to be a bit marginal: this view is certainly reinforced by the racers and their need for outboard bearings for the mainshaft to prevent (or contain) flex. In general road use the gearbox is reasonably reliable, but the layshaft bearings are weak. Symptoms of a failing layshaft bearing are roughness and the kick starter lever moving backwards when riding. Replacement of the bearing is straightforward, but the condition of the metal between the layshaft bearing and sleeve gear bearing should be carefully examined when the gearbox is out, since the case can crack between the two shafts. The sleeve gear bush can also wear, as may be seen from bronze filings in the oil. As a final comment on the gearbox, the kick starter pawls on pre-1971 bikes could break, but replacements are available.

The primary drive is pretty reliable and causes few problems. The main modification that can be made is the fitting of a toothed belt drive to replace the standard chain. Belt drives offer a smoother and quieter running drive that is more tolerant of sprocket misalignment than the standard Triplex chain, and are largely maintenance-free. A belt drive enables the drive to be run without oil, but it is well worth ventilating the primary chain case to ensure the alternator does not overheat.

Norvil belt kit fitted to a Mark 3.

Ignition System

Electronic ignition systems have a number of advantages over the standard system, but there are also three notable disadvantages. The first is that if something goes wrong it is almost impossible to fix it at the side of the road, although fortunately the systems seem to be pretty reliable. The second is that some systems are sensitive to battery voltage. Low voltages can cause erratic running and bad starting, so you may not be able to limp home, as you may do with an original system. The Commando, however, has a robust and reliable charging system as standard, and it can be upgraded using modern electronics, so this issue is easily addressed. The third is that the Boyer and Sparx systems do not allow for independent adjustment of the timing of each cylinder as the rotor magnets and pickups are fixed. However this does not seem to be a problem, presumably as the units are precision made, so are accurate out of the box.

In the author's view the many advantages outweigh the disadvantages. All the commercially available modern electronic ignition systems are reliable 'fit and forget' items that usually work straight from the box and require virtually no maintenance, with no wearing parts to replace. There are no points to close up and change the timing or corrode and kill the spark, and no mechanical advance retard unit to wear out and alter the advance curve characteristics. This does mean there is less excuse to go and fettle the bike, but on balance this is a good thing. Once an electronic system is fitted and the engine timing set, it will stay in tune unless disturbed.

Finally the cost: a Boyer or Sparx system (both used by the author) costs little more than renovating a mechanical ignition system. At the time of writing there is a shortage of points plates and mechanical advance retard units in good condition, although new springs are available, so if owners cannot refurbish their existing ones or find second-hand items they have a problem.

Sparx ignition stator plate as fitted to the 750 Commando restored in Chapter 6 : a 'fit and forget' solution.

If the twin leading shoe front brake is fitted, then the stiffening kit will make the brake more rigid and effective.

Braking

The Commando came with an 8in diameter twin leading shoe front drum until 1972, when a hydraulically operated disc brake was gradually introduced across the range. The rear brake was a 7in single leading shoe drum unit until 1975; this was replaced by a hydraulic disc brake on the Mark 3. The Commando is a fast bike and the brakes have come under a great deal of scrutiny over the years. A large number of improvements can be made to the front unit.

The drum brake is pretty good as drum brakes go, but is outclassed by the later disc unit. At least the drum is an alloy unit with a shrunk-in steel liner, which means good heat dissipation. The brakes fitted between 1969 and 1971 suffered from a relatively flexible brake plate, which meant braking performance was not as good as it could have been.

A stiffening kit, comprising a steel plate that sat behind the brake shoes and was fixed to the pivot pins and expanders, was produced for 1972 and is a good retro fit to earlier brakes. Other ways of improving the drum are to make sure that all the pivots are in good condition and lightly lubricated, the cable is a heavy duty item and the brake shoes are of the right compound for the type of riding. You should also chamfer the leading edge of each shoe to give more feel and stop the brake grabbing.

The standard 10.7in (27cm) diameter disc brake stops the bike adequately and is an improvement over the drum, but the lever pressure required to operate it is too high and the brake lacks feel. This is due to the bore of the master cylinder being too large for the size of the calliper. The problem can be cured by getting the standard calliper sleeved down to ⅝in. However, the brake is still relatively small in comparison to modern brakes and the calliper is also quite outdated, with a limited choice of brake pads. The Production Racer used a Lockheed racing calliper and offered single or twin discs. A number of retailers offer a variety of combinations of new discs in 12, 13 or 14in (30.5, 33 or 35.5cm) diameters and single or twin callipers, so there is a wide choice.

A fairly standard upgrade to the front brake: the Lockheed calliper with a larger diameter disc.

Norvil's take on the ultimate brake upgrade: twin large diameter discs with Lockheed callipers.

A slightly more extreme front brake upgrade: the twin piston Brembo calliper with large diameter disc.

If you want to be different, a set of Japanese forks with twin discs can be grafted onto the Commando.

Electrical Improvements

The Commando was introduced when British electrics had gone through the change from 6 volts to 12 volts and from magneto to coil ignition. It came equipped with a reliable and robust set of electrical equipment: a 12 volt alternator with Zener diode voltage control and reasonably robust and simple wiring and switches. As the bikes' electrics became more sophisticated with indicators, more powerful headlamps and eventually electric starters, the alternator was uprated to meet the additional load. A Commando with a standard electrical system is capable of running reliably for many miles.

Upgrades can be made to the generating side, the rectifying and regulating area and to specific items, such as the electric starter motor.

The alternator is the ubiquitous Lucas item with six coils on a static stator bolted into the primary chain case, which is energized by a magnetic rotor fixed to the end of the crankshaft. Originally the Commando was fitted with a Lucas RM21 unit, which produced 120 watts: on the JPN and the Mark 3 the alternator was updated using a Lucas RM23 180 watt unit with dual Zener diode charge control. On the early models the alternator stators did not have encapsulated coils. Such bikes would now be prone to having the insulation in the coil wire breaking down, leading to reduced output, but it is very unlikely that any of these stators are still in use.

There are now higher output alternators available, all of which have encapsulated coils on the stator, including three-phase units that produce 210 watts. Many of the newer alternators will produce higher power at given revs than the standard Lucas variants.

In addition to the alternators, standard plate type Lucas rectifiers are getting old and can be cheaply replaced by solid state units, the most common being a small square unit with four spade terminals on one face. These units usually have the additional advantage of consuming less power in operation. Finally, solid state

The three-phase alternator fitted to the restored 750 has three wires that feed into a regulator rectifier mounted on the back of the air filter.

Factory Customs: Commando Hi-Rider and Triumph Hurricane

The 1970s saw a proliferation of 'factory custom' machines from the big four Japanese factories and even one from BSA-Triumph, a strange phenomenon bearing in mind that a custom machine was supposed to be one modified by its owner. Norton, however, has a real claim to being the first manufacturer to introduce a factory custom with its Hi-Rider model, which was introduced to a frankly incredulous public (in the UK at least) in 1971.

Even though it was essentially a parts bin special, the Hi-Rider predated the Triumph X75 Hurricane by two years and was way ahead of the Japanese customs of later years. The Hurricane was the last new model produced by BSA-Triumph before their shotgun marriage to Norton, and was their first stab at the custom market. Designed by Craig Vetter, a young American designer, the Hurricane was based on the BSA Rocket 3. It was originally designed during 1970 and, in contrast to the Hi-Rider, used a large number of non-standard parts to achieve the desired custom appearance. The Hurricane had extended fork stanchions that compromised high-speed stability, wore a unique and very stylish one-piece glass fibre seat and tank unit, special headlamp mounts not unlike those used on the 1950s Gold Star, a special cylinder head with extended cooling fins to give a 'big, tough' look (in Vetter's words), and had a unique exhaust system with three individual chromed pipes

The Craig Vetter-designed Triumph Hurricane, produced in 1973, was based on the BSA Rocket 3.

leading to three silencers stacked one above the other on the drive side. In addition to all the special parts, the BSA Rocket 3 itself had gone out of production in 1972 when the entire BSA range was dropped, so the underlying frame and engine used by the Hurricane was already obsolete when the limited production run of about 1,000 bikes was produced for the 1973 sales season.

While the Hurricane certainly looked the part and was much more radical than the Hi-Rider, its use of parts that were unique to the model, and the obsolete Rocket 3 frame and engine, would have meant disruption to the Trident production line and high costs for the relatively small production run. In contrast, by using the standard frame and forks for the Hi-Rider, the traditional Commando handling was not compromised and, by dipping into the parts bin, the chopper custom look was achieved at minimal cost and disruption.

The most distinctive feature of the Hi-Rider was its ape hanger handlebars. Other changes were limited to a humped seat with a unique grab rail-cum-sissy bar, a small 5¾in diameter headlight and a small 2 gal fuel tank from the SS model. It must be said that the Hi-Rider was not such a radical departure as the Hurricane, and was not held in such high esteem, then or now. If you are in the market for a British factory custom you pay your money and make your choice: expensive, radical Hurricane or the cheaper, less extreme Hi-Rider. As the first of the breed and being a Commando, though, it is easy to build your own Hi-Rider.

Norton's earlier Hi-Rider appeared in 1971 and was less radical than the Hurricane. The ape hangers and sissy bar on the seat were very 'Easy Rider'.

A single seat and tank unit was the Hurricane's trademark styling feature, along with the three silencers stacked up on the right-hand side.

Another extensively modified Commando, pictured at the Fleet Carnival meet in 2009.
This Spanish registered 850 has uprated brakes, revised handlebars and after market
rear suspension units, among other modifications.

'black box' combined regulator and rectifier units are available to replace the rectifier and Zener diode, often at a cost that is less than replacing both components. The three-phase alternator units come with a dedicated regulator rectifier black box.

There is much debate on how to improve the electric starter on the Mark 3. This can be split into improving the electric start motor itself and improving the electric power getting to it. The starter motor can be modified to four-brush standard using Prestolite components listed in the INOA Tech Digest, which makes the motor more powerful. Replacing the battery for a larger capacity unit is a good start, but this can mean replacing the Mark 3 carrier and air filter assembly with an earlier unit to create room. All of the starter wiring should be replaced, especially the starter cables that connect the battery to the starter via the solenoid, and the starter and battery earth leads, using leads that are as heavy duty as possible to cut resistance.

Like any electrical system, clean and corrosion-free switches and connections will go a long way towards ensuring a strong and reliable system.

Owning a Norton

Pete Isted's 1975 850 Commando Interstate Mark 3, Late 1970s

While he was studying Marine Engineering in Liverpool in the late 1970s, Pete Isted ran a Commando Interstate Mark 3 for a year. He bought it because he was not interested in going Japanese after his reliable 1968 Triumph Bonneville, so the Commando seemed to be the next logical step up the British motorcycling hierarchy and it had the right amount of cachet he was looking for. Pete felt that it gave him

Pete Isted's 850 Interstate Mark 3 pictured in the late 1970s. Fork gaiters were standard on the UK Mark 3s and the large tank enabled Pete to ride from Hampshire to Liverpool in one hit.

Pete's Mark 3 was totally standard. The bike performed well and was reliable and comfortable.

Pete on his Mark 3.

increased power, reliability, superior handling and the ability to cover long distances in comfort at speed. It was in excellent condition when he bought it, with one previous owner who had obviously looked after it. The bike was used to transport Pete from his home in Yateley, Hampshire, to Liverpool, a one-way trip of some 220 miles of mixed motorway and A roads, and for commuting from his digs into college daily in the urban environs of Liverpool. The bike handled this varied usage competently, and gave Pete no major problems in the year that he owned it – until the extra performance of a customized Kawasaki Z900 became irresistible.

The bike was very comfortable, with a good riding position, thick and well-padded seat and an excellent handlebar bend, all factors that made riding a pleasure. The bike also handled beautifully, making the relatively long journey from home to college enjoyable. The large tank and decent fuel economy of around 60mpg (4.7ltr/100km) meant he could do the trip in one hit without having to stop for fuel or comfort breaks. Throw-over panniers and a top box and aftermarket rack gave Pete the luggage-carrying capacity he needed, and did not seem to upset the bike even when fully loaded. With the bike in constant use, the electrics never gave any trouble

and the electric starter actually worked the way the makers intended. The only downside of his time with the bike was when he dropped it on a diesel-soaked roundabout. He can still remember the feeling of the bike sliding along the road on its side and bashing into the kerb. Luckily there was little damage to Pete and only a dented fuel tank and bent handlebars on the bike. Pete had to push the bike to a garage and bent the handlebars straight before continuing his journey with the bike showing a definite bias to the right.

Pete and the author recall one incident when they went to Ken Heanes in Fleet, the local Triumph/BSA/Norton dealer, who still stocked some spares even though his main business by the late 1970s was in various Japanese models. Pete parked the Commando on the forecourt next to a Triumph Trident T160, the electric-start model contemporary to the Commando Mark 3. We came out of the shop at the same time as the Trident pilot and there was an interested crowd around the two classic (or were they just old-fashioned in those days?) British bikes. As Pete mounted the Commando, the murmur from the crowd was that the Commando wouldn't start but the Trident would. Pete thumbed the button, and the Commando instantly burst into life on the electric starter and settled down to its usual 800rpm tick-over, with the whole bike shuddering gently. The Trident rider pressed his button, the Trident coughed but nothing happened. Twice he tried, but the bike wasn't having any of it – and the Triumph rider had to kick the recalcitrant beast into life. He rode off without acknowledging us, and the crowd was just a bit puzzled at this reversal of perceived knowledge.

The author also remembers some rides on the pillion. The outstanding memory was of the comfort of the bike: the long seat gave plenty of room and was well padded, the pillion footrests were perfectly positioned for those over 6ft tall and the rear grab rail was large and easy to find. Probably the best feature was the lack of vibration, except for some shuddering at low revs. It was an excellent bike and Pete, who now lives in Australia and rides a heavily modified Harley-Davidson, still remembers it with affection.

Keith Glassborow's Modified 750 Commando Café Racer

Keith Glassborow has owned his Commando since 1998 and in that time has rebuilt virtually every component to get the bike just how he wants it. He is an excellent example of the type of Commando owner who is not afraid to alter and improve the bike, taking advantage of the huge range of improvements available to the enthusiast owner.

Keith's bike is approximately a 1973 model, but it was actually built up from bits in Café Racer style by the previous owner but one in 1977, and was ultimately converted to 'standard' Roadster style by the last owner after many years as a fully faired tourer. Keith bought it in April 1998 to use as a fun machine, but it needed some time to get it sorted and reliable, so at first he covered only between 700 and 1,000 miles per year.

Since Keith got it properly sorted in 2002, it has been reliable and is used for longer runs of up to 300 miles in a day. He modestly says this is nothing to shout about compared to some owners, but it is enough for him. The longest trip he has made was the 300-odd miles to Donnington in 2009 for the Norton Owners Club fiftieth anniversary meet. Since 2002 he has covered about 3,500 miles a year, with a total mileage of about 26,000 in his ten years of ownership. During this time he has found that the best help has come from forums, especially Jerry Doe's Norton Commando site (for further details see the Bibliography). As far as Keith is concerned, the information on this US site and the people who use it are second to none. Within the UK, Keith has much praise for Mick Hemmings and Roger at RGM, who offer straightforward advice and are good to deal with, as is Nick Hopkins at Andover

Keith Glassborow on his much modified 1973 750 Commando.

When bought by Keith Glassborow the bike was a standard-looking roadster in Black and Gold.

Norton.

The bike looked and sounded good when Keith bought it, but had obviously been treated to a cosmetic paint job. When Keith started to scratch the surface he found it to be, in his own words:

> a shed, the classic art of bodge was everywhere. Everything that could be reached with a paintbrush without removing parts had been touched up in black or silver. Both oil and petrol tanks were cushioned with carpet offcuts as was the rotten seat pan. The fuel tank was only mounted by the front studs, one of which was fractured and leaking.

The list went on and on. The fuel tank was also rusting from the inside, and rust particles were clogging up the carbs; this was only fixed when Keith sealed the tank with epoxy. The forks were full of water, and the wiring harness was shot with lots of connectors hanging on by a few strands of wire. The wheel rims were rusting, rear shocks were knackered, frame tubes were crushed by fairing brackets, the Isolastics were shot, the rear cush drive inserts were scrap, and the bike weaved and steered to the left. And that was just the running gear: the exhaust system used 850 Mark 3 pipes with the balance pipes capped off, the silencers were mismatched (1¼in on one side and 1½in on the other). The engine had a few issues:

> The engine cases had been welded after dropping a valve, I was told, and metal filler used to fill the gap at the rear where they did not meet! (I had to replicate this on the first rebuild). The front crankcase stud was just holding on failing threads which needed helicoiling. The cylinder head was good except for stripped main stud threads, and the Steve Maney alloy barrels were good bore-wise but also had a poor centre thread. The pistons were good; the bores were standard as was the crank, and all in good nick.

The main bearings were OK but during the winter rebuild I found a lot of aluminium particles in the oil and filter. It transpired that these had come from cut-up Coke cans which had been used to shim the crank end float behind the bearings (wrong way). The bearings were also turning in the cases and were shredding the shims. The camshaft was supposedly a 2S but the previous owner had told me to time it differently from stock as the keyway was out of spec to the lobes. This had been supplied by a Norton specialist, now closed. Basically it had standard timing with 2S lift and was closest to spec if I timed it per the book, not as advised. Needless to say both carburettors were knackered.

The good news was that the gearbox was essentially a 1957 Dominator item with Commando mainshaft and was generally OK but the first and second gears were showing tooth pitting. These were replaced, as were the gearbox bearings.

In addition to this mechanical work, in the first year Keith also had the frame, cradle and miscellaneous parts powder coated, spraying the tank and side panels Fiat yellow. At the end of the year he rebuilt the engine with new bearings and rings, and at the same time reground the valves. The forks were rebushed, rear shocks renewed and the seat pan was welded and the seat recovered. Everything else, including the fork yoke and small brackets, was repainted by Keith with spray cans. The gearbox was fitted with new bearings and bushes, and new Surflex clutch plates were installed.

Once he had the bike back on the road, running reasonably and looking presentable, Keith could start to modify it to his own preferences. The bike has had an eventful life since then, including a major blow-up in 2002 that resulted in a complete rebuild, and a change from a standard roadster configuration to a Production Racer lookalike. The modifications made to the bike are many and varied and have been driven by a desire to get the bike to exactly how Keith wants it.

At first Keith found that the bike had a delightful habit of steering left and weaving at

Keith Glassborow's 750 as purchased: while it looked as if it was in good condition, there were a few issues.

speed. This was eventually traced to the rear Iso-lastic cradle and front mount being out of line. This was fixed in 2006 by having them both machined and the front aligned with a spacer to get the same offset front and rear: previously the engine and gearbox were slightly twisted relative to the frame and front wheel. The frame has had some remedial work since the 2002 blow-up, when it needed to be straightened, and was again powder coated in 2006. The fuel tank and side panels have been black, yellow, black and are now in the 1975 JPS No. 10 scheme. Keith did all the painting himself, using both aerosols and proper equipment, depending on the availability of suitable paint (he recently found a new source of cellulose). He finds that a good finish is easy provided the final coats are colour sanded, lacquered, sanded and compounded.

The front forks have been rebuilt twice, the second time with dual rate springs and a Covenant anti-top conversion. Keith has also found that using 10/40 engine oil in the forks rather than ATF improved the ride and stopped most of the topping out, although the recent John Bould insert conversion is tempting.

The brakes are a standard rear drum, which functions quite well, while the front has a standard calliper, a ½in RGM sleeved master cylinder and a drilled standard disc (eighty holes, giving a saving of 12oz) that stops the bike well: it's not a two- or three-finger job but he is happy with it. The calliper came with stainless pistons and he uses EBC pads.

The original rims were past their sell by date when he bought the bike, so the wheels were rebuilt by Central Wheel in Coleshill with steel rims and stainless steel spokes, and fitted with the usual Avon AM20/21 combination in 90/90 and 110/90 sizes. Since then Keith has got through two more rears and, after a second Bridgestone rear, is now on AM26 at both ends. The Bridgestones helped solve the tram-lining to which he

An extreme version of the Norton Smile: Keith Glassborow's 750 engine after a connecting rod bolt let go. Cases and con rod are scrap.

Keith Glassborow resprayed the bike in Fiat yellow, which is a close approximation to the Norvil shade. The bike was starting to be sorted here.

found the AM20 front was prone and the new AM26s have retained the improvement. He gets around 4,000 miles on the rear before they start to square off. The fronts, of course, last at least 10,000 miles. At the end of 2007 he rebuilt the wheels himself with Akront shouldered aluminium rims.

The bike's engine was rebuilt on a budget in late 1998 with new rings, bearings and a valve job. This engine lasted 6,000 miles before a 'new' con rod bolt let go at 70mph in October 2002. The resulting damage – wrecked cases, barrels, left-hand side con rod, and a bent cam – also bent the front Isolastic bolt and the frame rails leaving the left-hand mount 7mm further forward than the right. This engine had also suffered the 1972 model issues of poor oil return at high speed due to Norton locating the pickup at the front of the crankcases for this year. The previous owner had blocked the large rear breather and located an 850-style part in the timing case as well as drilling the required three holes in the timing crankcase.

Keith believes that if the breather had been left as standard it would have been OK, the consensus being that the ½in pipe returned as much if not more oil than the pump itself! In early 2002 Keith had modified the location of the pickup back to the rear of the cases after suffering an empty oil tank on several occasions. Whether that contributed to the engine's demise is hard to say, since it never reached the stage where it was rattling with zero oil pressure. He had lived with the problem by keeping the continuous revs under 4,000rpm. The rod bolt was 3,000 miles old when it failed and Keith thinks that it was probably just bad luck, although it broke right where Paul Dunstall's Tuning Notes advises that new bolts should be polished to remove turning marks, which were fortunately absent on the new bolts.

Following the blow-up, a set of good Gus Kuhn stamped 850 cases was sourced from RGM and rebuilt with new rods, 850-style 750 bored barrels, pistons and a standard cam with

Keith Glassborow's 750 is now configured as a Production Racer lookalike.

reground followers: that was costly! Early in 2006 the head was rebuilt with new seats and a Serdi valve job (no manual valve grinding needed) by the Cylinder Head Shop. Keith feels that this was money well spent as an excellent job was done. When Keith rebuilt the engine in 2002 he fitted a standard cam. He likes the result but he does miss the extra pull of the old '2S', which really came in at 4,500rpm. He would like to try the PW3 and that could be on the next Christmas list.

After the original rebuild in 1998, the bike was basically reliable, apart from the gear change quadrant detaching itself from its pivot, jamming the box in third gear, and a propensity to swing the kick-start in first gear. However this was not the result of a failing layshaft bearing, which had been replaced with a roller, but was found to be caused by end loading of the kick-start shaft and second gear dogs. This was finally cured with a high specification ball bearing on the drive side and carefully placed spac-

ers on the drive side. In addition the layshaft timing side was converted to take a needle race.

Initially Keith ran the primary drive as standard with the chain and lubricated it with ATF. He later converted to a Norvil belt drive that has completed 18,000 miles. It does take a little work to get the pulleys running parallel, but it settled down after a period when the belt created a lot of rubber dust. A second LH gearbox adjuster was fitted recently as a precaution against the box twisting out of parallel. Keith definitely recommends belt drive conversion to cure leaks and he finds it seems to soften the transmission. He also thinks it is a good idea to vent the cases to keep the alternator stator cool, since without cooling oil he did manage to fry a Wassell replacement. The bike now has a Sparx stator item with drilled aluminium sheet over the inspection holes. An electronic rectifier/regulator from Paul Goff has cured overcharging and regular battery top-ups.

In the early days the clutch was very light (one finger) with 4 steel, 4 Surflex and the thick pressure plates, but it was always difficult getting neutral. When Keith realized most of the transmission was Dominator-based he sourced a set of inner and outer Commando gearbox covers with clutch operating mechanisms. In due course he found the Commando clutch arm gave more travel but required more force. This improved the neutral finding, but what cured it was replacing the diaphragm spring. The old one had uneven finger heights when totally dismantled and was not releasing evenly. These days it's a two-finger clutch that never slips. Finally Keith has had the front and rear sprockets machined to take a 520 'O' ring chain, which has reduced maintenance and constant chain adjustment. He recommends this conversion if the bike is used hard.

Having been a Roadster for most of its time with Keith, he was getting tired of being buffeted by the wind at motorway speeds, of being pushed back in the seat and of the generally uncomfortable riding position at higher speeds. At the end of 2006 he added RGM stainless clip-ons, Hemmings rear-set footrests and an old Production Racer fairing, restored to use with Hemmings Norvil mounts. The Production Racer riding position made the bike much more comfortable, apart from the inevitable wrist ache at low speed. Keith now finds that at above 65mph the riding position is fine and it makes good progress into a stiff headwind a lot more agreeable.

Perhaps the most memorable of the many great rides he has done would have to be the Brighton Burnup from the Ace Café in September 2008. The experience of being among the thousands of bikes pouring into Brighton, with people cheering and waving on bridges and at the roadside from the A40 to the A23, will stay with Keith for a long time.

The worst time has to be when the engine exploded at 70mph in October 2002. He was able to find and retrieve most of the debris while waiting for the recovery van at the side of the road. Keith found it a strange experience as there no bang as one might have expected, just a tinkling noise from the engine that sounded more like a broken spoke hitting the forks.

The slim lines of the Commando are shown to advantage in this rear shot of Keith Glassborow's 750.

The single-seat, John Player Norton stripe paint job and Production Racer fairing on Keith Glassborow's 750 combine to make a bike that is unmistakably a Commando.

Despite this, Keith is still riding and fettling the Commando. It is a bike that has got under his skin and gives him a great deal of pleasure in riding, maintaining and improving it.

Ken Rawlinson's Mark 3 and Production Racer

Ken Rawlinson currently owns two Commandos: a largely standard Mark 3 Interstate and a John Player Production Racer replica, which he has built up from parts sourced through autojumbles and eBay, and is based on the works John Player Production Racers of 1972 and 1973.

Ken has had his 828cc Norton Interstate Commando since he bought it new for about £1,150 from Elite Motors of Tooting, south-east London, in 1976. He bought the Norton as he wanted a new bike and Elite Motors was selling off Commandos and Triumph T160s cheaply due to the collapse of Norton Villiers Triumph. He really wanted a T160 because he then preferred the look of them, but they had all been sold. The salesman told him that the Commando was a better bike, as it was more reliable and had better fuel consumption, so he bought one. One problem arose while running in – an oil leak due to a porous barrel – but this was replaced under guarantee.

Ken Rawlinson's very original Mark 3 Interstate retains its original paint.

He has now done about 30,000 miles on the bike and reckons this is about right, as the only recurring problem with the bike has been three broken speedo cables, as well as the speedo gearbox going. This has happened twice while Ken has been on his way to the Isle of Man TT races, so he reckons to have to add about 2,000 miles to the recorded mileage. Apart from that it has been pretty reliable. Ken fitted a Boyer electronic ignition system to keep the timing consistent and avoid having to maintain the original points system. Other than changing worn out consumables such as chains, tyres, cables, batteries, silencers and, only recently, the exhaust pipes, the only major items Ken has had to change are the primary chain at about 25,000 miles (apparently this should be changed before 20,000 miles) and the carburettors. This again happened at 25,000 miles, but Ken feels that they should be really be changed before 20,000 miles since the poor quality Mark 1 Amal Concentrics wear out very quickly.

The worn-out carburettors assisted in providing Ken with a set of faults that were difficult to diagnose. He was getting a misfire after about 23,000 miles and thought that this was down to a faulty Boyer ignition system that he had fitted some while back, so he bought another but still had the misfire. He was then told that it was probably worn-out carburettors, so he bought and fitted a Mikuni but still had the misfire. Les Emery of Norvil Motorcycles told him to get rid of the Mikuni and go back to Concentrics, as 'the Norton knew what they were doing': the pair he bought, however, did not fix the misfire although it was a bit better. He set off for a Norton rally in the Lake District one sunny Friday morning from his home in south London but only got as far as Epsom when it started badly misfiring, as he describes:

I was rather angry but had stopped outside a very nice pub (funnily enough my bikes nearly always break down at or near pubs) so decided to console myself with a pint. I then struggled to get the bike home and thought I must find the fault. Finding that I had a very weak and then no spark, I contacted Boyer who told

Ken Rawlinson's Commando is set up for long-distance touring and has proved to be more than capable in this role. Ken found that the small fly screen improved the bike's comfort.

The underseat layout shows just how original the bike is. The factory toolkit is still in its pouch and the factory stickers are still in position.

me to make some checks which I did and found that the 'brand new' Boyer was faulty.

In conclusion the original fault was worn-out carburettors; I then changed the Boyer and got a faulty unit, so I now had two faults, which was why I had trouble finding them. If I had initially changed the carbs, I would have saved a lot of money. I should have noticed that the carbs were worn as the fuel consumption had dropped from the normal mid-50s mpg to mid 40s.

Ken also found that the front brake was very bad. While it would slow him down at first, it would then fade badly. No matter how hard you put the brake on it would still keep going. After twice almost running into the back of cars, he changed the front brake to an RGM unit with a Grimica calliper and had the master cylinder sleeved down. He also also changed the front disc for a larger RGM unit.

Apart from that the bike is all original. The engine, apart from the barrel, and gearbox have not been stripped down and the paintwork is also all original. Ken has considered getting some paintwork done but it is fine and has 'patina'.

Ken considers that the top speed is not brilliant and thinks that it would struggle to get past 110mph, but as far as he can remember he has not tested it to that extent. The great thing about the bike is that it will happily cruise at around 80–85mph with not too much stress to the rider. He did fit a small handlebar screen to the bike, however, as he would be making a long trip to Austria in 2009 and was finding that the wind pressure was too much after he broke his collarbone in a crash on his Triumph ST Sprint.

He has had many good times with the Commando but the highlight was probably the trip to Austria in July 2009 for the Norton Owners Club rally, which included taking it for a high speed 'tour' around the Salzburgring, near Salzburg.

He does not recall any particular 'worst moments' on the Commando but there was a honeymoon trip from Croydon to Aberdeen in a very snowy blizzard after having married on 1 April! Apparently no-one in Aberdeen believed that he and his new wife would make the journey in such appalling weather – the snow there was about six inches deep – so the friends they were meeting went out for the evening. Despite the distance and the inclement weather, however, the Commando behaved perfectly.

Ken's second Commando is a John Player Production Racer replica and is a completely different kettle of fish to his Interstate. It took several years to get the bike to its present state on the road. The bike is based on the works John Player Production Racers of 1972–73 and has been built up from parts bought on eBay and at autojumbles. The 850cc engine currently fitted is the actual Jim Boughen-tuned engine fitted to the 1974 Gus Kuhn bike that Geoff Barry rode to fourth place in the Isle of Man, and with which the late Dave Potter won a production race at Brands Hatch and also came fourth at Silverstone, even though he had a misfire. Ken had bought and raced this same bike, but much later sold it to the National Motorcycle Museum. The replica bike has been re-registered with the DLVA and now runs on a 1972 plate.

Ken has ridden the bike only a few hundred yards, since it is difficult to start, and he has mainly taken it to shows. The bike is an ongoing project. The one thing Ken is not too happy with is the exhaust system, as the bends in the pipes are not quite right: they are not as tight as the works pipes and don't look quite right to him.

Ken also has a highly tuned Mick Hemmings 750cc engine and a Quaife five-speed box, both as originally fitted to the JPN Nortons, which he intends to fit as soon as possible and then use the bike more on the road. He acknowledges that, with the clip-ons and rear sets, it is not an easy ride in Croydon's traffic and he would prefer it to have mirrors, but the bike certainly looks the business!

Ken Rawlinson's PR replica is built up from spares, although you would not guess it from looking at it.

Ken Rawlinson built the bike based on the 1972–73 John Player Norton team Production Racers. It is a faithful and well-executed replica, apart from the bend of the exhaust pipes.

The riding position of Ken Rawlinson's PR replica is possibly a bit extreme for town traffic.

Les Ward's 1972 Commando Interstate

Les Ward, the dating officer of the AMC Owners Club, and his friend Ken were at the Kempton Autojumble in spring 1994 when he came across a bright yellow Commando. Although the Commando had been his dream bike since he was sixteen years old, he decided to pass on it as he already had a couple of other bikes. He made the mistake, however, of owning up to his dream: Ken, cheerful soul that he is, said 'one day you'll be old and decrepit, sitting in the old folks home, mumbling about never having had a Commando', and he set me thinking. If I didn't buy it, I'll always regret missing the chance. So I bought it. Les has owned the bike ever since and uses it for long-distance touring, often on the Continent, on club runs and for general pottering around.

The bike is a 1972 Interstate with some modifications that were there when he bought it, while Les has been responsible for others. The bike retains the early Interstate specification low exhausts, so throw-over panniers can be fitted. The fitment of peashooter silencers improves the looks of the exhaust without compromising the luggage-carrying capability. The bike also has Boyer electronic ignition and Powerbox to provide sparks and charge and a single Mikuni carburettor. Mechanically, Les has not had to touch the motor since he bought the bike and as far as he knows it is standard (that is to Combat specification). He had to rebuild the gearbox, however, when the layshaft bearing failed at the end of his road after one of his long trips to France – the classic symptom of the kick starter lever moving

Les Ward has owned his 1972 750 Commando Interstate since 1994, since when he has used it for long-distance touring, including Continental trips.

The Interstate tank gives Les Ward the range he needs. He finds the bike comfortable and reliable.

down was the first sign that something was badly wrong. The gearbox was rebuilt with new bearings and there have been no further problems, except for the occasion when the gear lever fell off on the post-rebuild test drive and Les had to negotiate the last five miles home in top gear, which if anything demonstrated the engine's flexibility and the clutch's ability to take some punishment.

A second problem was caused by the Mikuni carburettor. This initially caused what seemed to be a clutch problem, with a very bad change between gears while in motion. Les eventually tracked the problem down to the suction from the engine jamming the carburettor slide and not allowing it to close fully when the twist grip was released. The carburettor now runs with three springs in its slide – the standard Mikuni, an Amal Concentric and a thin Moto Guzzi one. This makes the throttle close properly and the gear change reverted back to its usual slick self once the slide actually went back all the way down. The Mikuni is easier to tune than the twin Amals and gives better fuel consumption, which aver-

ages around 50–60mpg (5.7–4.7ltr/100km), giving a good 300 mile range from the Interstate tank. The carburettor does need the choke on for a long time before the bike warms up properly. Les has tried a number of different tyre combinations. When purchased it was shod with Dunlop TT100s, but he felt that they tended to fall into corners and changed them for the old-fashioned Avon Roadrunners, which he liked a lot. He later fitted more modern Avon AM20/AM21s. Initially he disliked these but grew to like them after a while, appreciating the grip and traction they provided, and felt that they were slightly better than the Roadrunners. He is presently back on Roadrunners but is planning to return to the AM20/AM21s once the existing tyres wear out.

Les finds that the bike handles better than he can ride, and he loves the bags of torque available in every gear and especially from low revs. The sensation as he opens the throttle and the bike gets up and goes is really special. While it has all the character of a British bike, he believes it is also capable of coping with modern traffic and will

One modification Les Ward has made to his early Interstate is the Mark 3 instrument panel mounted on the top yoke: easy to read and easy to get at the ignition switch.

potter down country lanes and cruise on motorways with equal repose. He also finds that it is capable of giving modern sports bikes a surprise on any road with some curves. One of Les's best moments on the bike occurred on a trip to France:

> The Sussex British Motorcycle Club used to hold a charity run on the Continent with 100 British bikes. I've great memories of early morning ferries. Dawn breaking on the horizon with a line of bikes ahead. Sunny spring days, when you stopped at a roadside café and watched the other Brit bikes roar past, or pull in to join you. Riding into the centre of Paris, with a Police escort waving you through the red traffic lights, stopping all the other traffic. Watching my mate Graeme stripping to his undies in a Calais car park to put on dry clothing because he'd said before the run, 'Do you think it's going to rain? Are you going to wear your waterproofs?' To which I'd replied, 'No. It looks fine to me'. I then changed my mind and poor Graeme was slightly annoyed by the time we had swum up to Calais. Magic moments all and I just have to see the old Commando to break into a smile. I'm

smiling now, as I'm off to Belgium next weekend [May 2010] to see Marc and the other lads from the Belgium British Bike Club, who I first met on one of these trips.

The changes from standard include the paint, which is an attractive Kawasaki Candy Apple red. Les now misses the leg pulling he used to get when the bike was yellow, including 'do you use custard for touch-up paint' and 'did they use paint or puke', and finds that he has to be careful not to damage the paint now that it looks so nice. So why does Les like the bike so much? Here are his last words on the subject:

> The all round ability. The grin on your face when you return home from a run. The fact that I know every nut and bolt on the bike. Really it's a two-wheeled symbol of enjoying life. Getting away from the pressures of life and work. Every ride is an adventure.

And that really does sum up all that is good about the Commando – a bike made for riding and enjoying.

Les Ward's Interstate is a fine example of a mostly original Commando still performing sterling service.

Tony Sumner's 1971 750 Commando: Shaken, but not Stirred

Tony Sumner was at school with the author and was probably the person who most fostered the author's love of British bikes. So here is his story of how he bought and ran his first Commando:

What do most men do to celebrate when their first child is born? Smoke a cigar? Savour a fine single malt whisky? Well, I don't smoke, and I've never much liked spirits.

So, in the summer of 1991, I bought a Commando.

To be totally honest, it wasn't quite as impetuous as that. FAF124L had been standing in the small row of second-hand bikes being sold on behalf of customers at Cambridge Motorcycles for some time, piquing my interest every time I walked in for a plug, an MOT or some cheery banter from Phil and Gary.

I'd been brought up on a diet of British twins and singles – Triumphs and Velos – so thoughts of oil leaks, starting rituals and Joe Lucas, the Prince of Darkness, did little to sway my enthusiasm. Schoolfriends Mike and Pete had had Commandos, a black 750 Roadster

and a silver 850 Mark 3 Interstate, and thoughts of a big, meaty twin with better handling, brakes and lights than my old sprung-hub Thunderbird, and with fewer oil leaks, vibration and starting issues than the Venom, seemed tempting.

Besides, the price seemed right and so, on 2 July 1991, and £1,150 lighter of pocket, I kicked my first Commando into life and burbled the mile from the industrial estate, past the Wrestlers pub, and home to evaluate my purchase.

What had my money bought me? Well, on the plus side, a rideable bike with reasonable starting, a healthy sounding engine, reasonable bodywork and a recently powder-coated frame, electrics that pretty much worked and no huge oil leaks. The bike had been first registered on 1 August 1972, and had nearly matching numbers frame and engine numbers: 153217 for the frame and 157217 for the engine. In the debit column there was the usual litany of entries and oddities in a typical twenty-year-old British twin's accounts. The tank and seat were in British Racing Green and fibreglass, the seat being Norvil, and the tank from a Fastback. The pipes and silencers

The 1971 750 Hi-Rider restored by the author is a controversial machine. People either love it or hate it!

were original and sound, but the chrome was tired and they were from an S-type. The café-racer tank and seat had been teamed with standard footrests and bars, which made for an interesting riding position, and the rear mudguard, air cleaner and sundry other small items were missing. The wiring, though working, made enthusiastic use of red cable, the front brake seemed poor after the Venom (but great after the Thunderbird) and the wheel rims and fork legs had been finished in white.

Putting the bike through a quick MOT the same day resulted in a failure for having a fibreglass fuel tank – despite it being (probably) the original one it shipped with. There was some ambiguity over the status of fibreglass tanks at that time, and a visit to a different test station produced the desired pass.

As the summer wore on I rode the bike to work and began a process of rolling restoration – not to factory-pristine state, but to the sort of Commando I'd always fancied – a cherry-red metallic Roadster.

The high bars and small tank of the Hi-Rider make it impractical at high speed and for long-distance riding. But as a cruiser the author has found it ideal.

Probably not the right colour for 1972, but always my favourite.

First job was to fit a points cover over the Boyer Bransden ignition triggers. The second was to strip off the excess white paint, which revealed surprisingly good rims but the usual Roadholder fork crack near the spindle pinch bolt. This had been repaired, but I found another slider as soon as possible. I found a new old stock Roadster tank in cherry-red metallic (and in steel …) and a right-hand side panel. Finding the left one to match took months, however. A new Roadster seat and rear mudguard were fitted, and the gaping Concentrics treated to a new air filter assembly. I eventually found some headlamp shrouds to replace the café-racer style ones fitted, and some Lucas indicators and pillion footrests were retrieved from an aborted project in the shed.

Fitting the indicators triggered an overhaul of the wiring. The pipes and silencers were replaced with new parts and my dad made up some silencer brackets in stainless steel. Finally, a new centre stand and all its associated gubbins were fitted, which was probably the trickiest job of the lot.

On the road, the Commando felt taut and stiff, a bit clinical and distant from the road when compared with the Venom, which, while it steered well, always felt a bit 'flexible': the difference, apart from geometry, I suppose, between a 1970s welded frame and a 1950s one made from a sequence of brazed tube and lugs.

Starting was fine but, because I'm five foot four and the seat was high, required some commitment to that push on the kick-start! The engine was what I had hoped for – smooth, powerful and responsive, and the clutch and box worked unobtrusively.

In the end, other projects, and a few niggles and mismatches between me and the bike, meant it had to go. I could never quite seal a persistent slight mist of oil from the rev counter drive. The seat was always a bit too tall for someone with my genetic makeup, and the twin Concentrics always made the twistgrip feel heavy in traffic, although nothing like, say, an early LeMans. Finally I was never happy with the front brake – I checked and replaced the linings, had it skimmed, carefully set up the linkages, and it still felt inadequate for the speed and weight of the bike, especially in modern traffic.

*The timing side of the restored Hi-Rider retains the classic Commando look.
The bars are surprisingly comfortable at legal speeds.*

When Ttony bought his Commando in 1991 it was somewhat removed from standard.

So, after a few thousand miles and despite the many fine qualities of the bike, including great spares availability at reasonable prices, FAF124L was sold.

Would I have another Commando? Well, if I came across a cherry-red metallic Mark 3 Roadster, with a working electric foot, an SU carb conversion and modern discs up front, I might be tempted.

Would I have another daughter? Well, I did, but I celebrated in a different way…

Another satisfied owner, I think!

My Riding Impressions

My 1971 Hi-Rider offers an interesting contrast to the traditional roadster or tourer Commando. At first glance it looks as if the high bars are completely impractical and the seat would be too short to be comfortable. My initial riding impressions show that the handlebars do not impinge on the riding experience at lower speeds, but they do make the rider feel like a parachute at higher speeds. As for the seat, it actually works very well for me, as the seat hump starts just where I want it and I sit against it. This stops me from sliding back along the seat, either by the acceleration or the wind pressure. My first impressions of the bike as I prepared to take it out for the first ride were of size. Not just the bars, but the seat height, the width of the seat, the distance between the foot rests and the length. My usual ride, a US specification 1970 Triumph Bonneville (pre-oil in frame) felt a lot smaller in comparison, especially on the width of the rear of the fuel tank, and the distance between the footrests and the seat. Interestingly the higher weight of the Commando did not make itself felt, either at a standstill or riding, presumably because it is all quite low down.

I am very impressed with the performance of the Commando's 750cc engine. It is much torquier than my Bonneville or 1965 BSA A65 Lightning, and is also very flexible. The gearbox is nice and smooth, and the clutch, once properly adjusted, is nice to use, reasonably light in operation and can handle the power without complaint. Acceleration in the intermediate gears is explosive, even while running in, and in top the bike will pull happily and quickly from under 2,000rpm. It is a real top gear

everywhere bike, with instant electrifying acceleration in reserve if you have to drop down a gear – even with the high bars. The bike is happy to cruise at 55–65mph and, although I'm running in, is happy to accelerate up to the UK legal limit of 70mph with no drama or effort – even with the built-in parachute of the rider hanging onto the high bars. Speeds above this would be uncomfortable, but the Hi-Rider was not designed for high speed scratching, so I can forgive the bike this quirk.

Handling is up there with the best. The bike will take a line and stick to it, and the suspension does not seem to be affected by any bumps or ridges in the road. Ground clearance is excellent: while I can ground my Bonnie's stand on left-handers, I've not had any problems so far with the Commando. The ride is currently a bit stiff and slightly choppy, but I suspect that as the suspension beds in this will disappear and the ride will smooth out – that's what happened to my Bonneville. Practicalities are good, the bike is easy to haul up onto its centre stand, and the side stand (remembering it is an aftermarket clamp on one that is welded to the lower frame tube) works well, but it is a trifle difficult to access as its end is under the drive-side footrest. The 6in headlamp with its modern Wipac reflector and 60/55 watt H4 halogen bulb works well, giving a good spread of light and clearly defined dip. The rear light and indicators all work, and the Sparx 3 phase alternator is up to the job of keeping the battery charged and the Sparx ignition firing reliably.

The most striking feature is the lack of vibration. There are some slight tremors through the footrests at 2,000 to 2,500rpm, but otherwise the bike is really smooth. The mirrors give a clear image of the road behind at all revs: this is something I've not experienced on a British bike before, having become used to interpreting the blurs on all my other bikes! While the bike is very smooth, the riding experience is not remote – the induction roar and exhaust note tell you that there is a traditional twin rumbling away downstairs and the acceleration emphasizes the point. The steel fuel tank also sets up a drumming resonance at some speeds, which indicates that I need to look at the mounts.

The Norvil PR-style seat sits uncomfortably with the Fastback tank, and the 'S' type exhaust system give the timing side a Spartan look.

Tony reconfigured the bike as a roadster, using a new old stock steel fuel tank in Cherry Red metallic paint.

As a Roadster, the bike gave Tony a lot of pleasure, but the tall seat height and drum front brake eventually forced him to sell it.

I have found only a couple of downsides so far. The steering lock is really poor, making it awkward to manoeuvre the bike around the yard or when parking. This is pretty minor, but the second is a bit more serious: the twin leading shoe drum front brake. As initially set up it was poor, and it ran out of adjustment very quickly when I first started to use the bike. I suspect that I had too much taken off the front hub when I had it skimmed, but did not have an option as I had to take out all the rust. I quickly replaced the hub with a second-hand item, however, and this transformed the brake. When properly set up, its performance seems to be acceptable, but not as good as the Triumph twin leading shoe brake on my Bonneville. I suspect that the stiffening kit is a major factor in the reasonable performance as the brake plate itself is pretty flimsy in comparison to the Triumph unit. However I feel that the brake is probably not up to the performance and weight of the bike. The rear brake works, although it is nothing to write home about, and seems to be bedding in nicely.

So in summary, while I like the bike a lot, I do think that I need to fit a front disc brake to give the bike the brakes needed to match its performance. As for keeping it as a Hi-Rider, I will see. I may change the bars for some slightly less extreme ones, but that would ruin the overall appearance, so I may just chop and change seats, tanks, headlamps and bars to suit the sort of riding I want to do at the time – just as the Norton method allows you to do. After all, there are very few Hi-Riders on the road and sometimes it's nice to be different. One final job I wanted to do now that the bike was running was show it to my father-in-law, Eddie Humfryes. He was a lifelong motorcycle fan but by then was too frail to ride. But he thoroughly enjoyed sitting on the bike and giving the throttle a bit of stick!

Conclusions

The high regard that current and previous owners have for the Commando shines through in all of these owners' accounts. Also notable is the way that the contemporary owners take advantage of the many ways of improving the Commando, ranging from the substitution of later Norton parts to the incorporation of new components. The main suppliers of Norton parts in the UK and USA are able and willing to assist an owner in identifying the parts that can be improved and will usually be happy to supply them. The owners clubs and various internet forums (see Recommended Suppliers and Bibliography below) are great sources of non-partisan information and advice. Finally the Norton Owners Club Service Notes and the INOA Tech Digest give details of these and other modifications that can be made to improve a Commando (for further details see the Bibliography). The Commando is probably unique in the UK classic scene as the bikes are still used for their intended purpose and the majority of owners do not pursue originality over practicality.

6 Restoration

First, a word about safety. The following chapter describes the methods and techniques I use to restore a bike. Anyone who embarks on such a project should be aware that there are dangers associated with working on old bikes: this warning is important as old oil, petrol and other fluids used in old bikes could be toxic, there is a strong likelihood that the brakes will have asbestos in the shoes and in the dust in the drums, and there is a constant risk of injury from sharp tools and bits of bike. Anyone who decides to restore their own bike should only attempt jobs that they are competent to do, and take all safety precautions that are needed. If in doubt, ask an expert.

Armed with knowledge on the Commando gained from reading books and magazines, I started to look for a suitable candidate for restoration. As I wanted to do a full restoration, which would help me in learning about the Commando as I wrote this book, I was not too concerned about condition, although I wanted to make sure that all the main components were there: frame, forks, engine, gearbox, wheels and, hopefully, some tin (or glass fibre) ware. This was so I could restore as much as possible rather than just replace missing bits: if all the parts originally came from the same bike then so much the better, as it would make it easier to get the bike registered in the UK. After I had been

As bought the 1971 Commando was in a bit of a state, although the only large parts missing were the seat and mudguards. The high handlebars were impressive.

With the engine and gearbox numbers matching the frame, the bike was original. The head came separately along with a couple of boxes containing most of the other smaller bits.

looking for a Commando project for a month or so, I had learnt a lot about the slightly strange market in which Commandos exist. There are very few cheap basket cases, as the Commando has a thriving second-hand spares market and any mostly complete bike seemed to be worth a lot more in bits than I wanted to pay! Interestingly the same issue had not arisen when I bought BSA and Triumph twins, and I imagine that it is down to the relative scarcity of the Norton product. I eventually found that Neil McCallum of Triples Workshop in Wakefield, Yorkshire, had a number of Commandos coming back from the USA, including a couple of basket cases that sounded interesting. The Commando I ended up with (to Neil's surprise) looked as if it had been left outside in a damp region of the US for several decades, but it seemed straight, the frame was not too rusty, it came with forks and wheels, and the engine, gearbox and primary drive were in the frame.

The downside was that the cylinder head was off and the pistons were firmly seized in the rusty bores. Neil also had most of the underseat gub-

bins – oil tank, battery carrier and the air filter end plate – along with a tank and side panels and the alloy 'Z' plate footrest assemblies, all with a healthy coating of rust and all supplied in the traditional slightly damp cardboard boxes. The final touch was an impressive set of 13in high ape hanger bars, just like those fitted to the Hi-Rider. The bike's Vehicle Identification Number (VIN) plate on the headstock showed the manufacture date as June 1971 and the frame, engine and gearbox numbers all matched. The number came from late 1971, so it all looked correct. The forks sported a Missouri Safety Inspection sticker dated in the first half of 1974 and the speedo showed 13,436 miles. This could well be the original mileage and the last time the bike was on the road, so it looked like it had only had about three years on the road: often US bikes were run for a couple of years then, when something went wrong, were dumped in the backyard and abandoned. Stripping and rebuilding showed not a huge amount of wear on most components, so I reckon that the mileage was correct.

Researching a Restoration

In order to carry out a restoration, I like to do lots of research on the target bike before purchasing. Many sources may be consulted, including buying original factory produced workshop manual(s), parts books and brochures, if possible. Original magazine articles and road tests of the model range also provide a good idea of what the press of the time thought of the bike, while articles in the current classic bike press give the 'real' picture.

The workshop manual tells you in detail how to take things apart and put them back together, along with the various specs and tolerances required, whereas the parts manual gives an exploded view of every part of the bike, with diagrams that show just about every component. The latter has three very important uses: it can help identify the obscure part in the bottom of the box of bits is (and perhaps clarify if it even belongs on the bike in the first place); it enables you to work out which parts make up which sub-assembly and hence what is actually missing; and it shows the order in which the parts need to be assembled to make up a sub-assembly, and where that sub-assembly fits on the bike.

Documentation can come from a number of sources. Autojumbles often have sellers who specialize in original sales brochures and documentation or who sell photocopies of originals. Bargains can be found from other stall holders with original brochures, parts books or workshop manuals sometimes scattered among the spare parts. The internet and specifically eBay throw up many original documents, as well as reprints and CDs with collections of documents copied onto them. Most of the specialist parts suppliers, such as Norvil and RGM, provide their own catalogues with price lists and often use the original Norton parts numbers. They also sell parts lists and workshop manuals.

The specialist parts seller's catalogues are particularly useful as they tell you what is available new and the price. During the restoration I had been happily scouring eBay for those elusive Commando bargains. It was somewhat enlightening to see second-hand parts going for more than good quality new parts: of special note was a stainless steel rear mudguard, which went for about 20 per cent more than Norvil or RGM would have charged. It is really useful to have a copy of one of their catalogues to hand to cost these things up and to set your maximum bid.

For the Commando there are also two books of useful hints and tips produced by various owners clubs: Commando Service Notes, written by Tim Stevens and John Hudson, edited by Alan Osborn and produced by the UK Norton Owners Club (NOC), and the Tech Digest edited by Michael Frick and produced by the International Norton Owners Association. The Tech Digest is available from the Norton Owners Club, but Commando Service Notes is no longer in print and I sourced my copy from eBay. When carrying out a restoration I always buy a modern photocopy of the relevant parts manual to use as a 'garage' version and copy the relevant pages from the workshop manual when needed for use in the garage. This avoids getting any more greasy fingerprints on the original documents bought off eBay. I also buy a stock of stainless nuts, bolts and washers for use during the restoration. The Commando uses mainly UNF nuts and bolts on the cycle parts, which are easily available and relatively cheap. The original nuts and bolts will usually be rusty: even if you get them recoated, they will eventually rust again. I want my restorations to stay looking good, so I use stainless where I can, and will also replace specialist parts with stainless if available.

Once I have purchased a bike, the first part of my restoration method is an initial assessment by planning and perusing parts lists and workshop manuals. Overall I aim to assess what I've got and work out what is missing before making a list of parts to hunt down. Once I've got an idea of what's what, I generally take the approach of first completing a rolling chassis (frame and fitting, wheels and suspension) done, then doing the mechanicals, the wiring and finally the painting. In any restoration, however, it is important to be flexible. As any good project manager knows, a plan must be flexible, and often it is useful to do jobs in parallel, or infill time doing jobs while you are waiting for something. In the restoration documented in this chapter, for example, I stripped down the engine while waiting for the frame to come back from the powder coaters as I had identified that there was going to be a major problem getting the seized pistons out of the barrels. This was done while the frame was away, saving time later. Look at the project as a whole and try to work out what order you need to do things in.

Dismantling

The first job was to get the carcass into the garage and set up so that it was convenient to work on. The bike had no stands and so needed to be hoisted up on my trolley-type lift. This allows the bike to be wheeled around, and gets both wheels off the ground. As a health and safety note, make sure the bike is securely fastened to the trolley. I use nylon tie-down straps to fix it on so it can't topple over when being pulling about or worked on. With the bike in place the initial strip-down could commence. The aim was to get down to a bare frame that could then be sent away for blasting and powder coating. First the seized pistons were given a good dose of penetrating oil and were then ignored while the wheels came off. The front wheel spindle came out easily – there was no wheel spindle nut, and the pinch bolt on the fork slider was also loose. The fork slider was undamaged – often on Norton Roadholders the alloy is cracked or broken if the pinch bolt was overtightened. The front brake arms were rusty and the tie rod was bent, so all were put on the 'replacements needed' list, along with a new rim and spokes since they were too rusty to save. Otherwise the alloy hub looked to be in good condition and the wheel bearings weren't too bad, but I replaced them anyway as a matter of course. The front tyre, part worn, was the originally fitted Avon GP type and the rear was a relatively unworn TT100, both of which helped to confirm the mileage at around 13,000. The front brake plate looked alright, but the internals were rusty and needed a good clean and an assessment of what needed replacement. The rear wheel was a bit more of a struggle, as the rear spindle was rusty and reluctant to slide through the spacer on the timing side. However it eventually relented after some gentle hammering with a rubber mallet. The wheel itself was firmly fixed to the hub, and again needed persuasion to let go. The rubbers in the hub that mated with the three drive lugs on the wheel had turned into a powdery mess and all but disappeared. Once the wheel was separated from the hub a large amount of dried grass showed where the mice had set up

residence! The hub and bearings were in good shape, while the rim and spokes were rusty and needed replacement.

With the wheels out it was time to get the forks off. The chrome on the top nuts was gone, and they were so badly pitted that they were beyond re-chroming, but both came out easily. The damper rods, which are screwed into the ends of the top nuts, also undid with no problem, freeing the instrument pods. The rusted-in Allen bolts in the bottom yoke freed up after a good dose of penetrating oil and, with the top nuts screwed back into the stanchions, both the fork legs came out of the yokes with a couple of light blows. While the yokes were covered in surface rust, there was original silver paint where the stanchions fitted. Both fork legs had oil in them and one had some water in it as well. On both legs the plastic dust excluders were very brittle and both had a length of green cloth under them, obviously to soak up oil leaking past the seals. With the fork legs out, I turned to the yokes, which on the 1971 models are held in place with a big nut on the lower end of the steering spindle. This nut proved to be rusty and very stubborn, and I used an air-powered impact driver to loosen it. With the yokes removed, I could then knock out the steering bearings. These were two sealed roller races with a spacer tube between them, and could be knocked out with a drift once the spacer tube was moved to one side. Both bearings were in really good condition and the spacer tube still had a coat of shiny black paint – the first bit of the bike that was in good condition!

All this had taken about a week, and all the time the seized pistons and bores had been stewing in their penetrating oil. I had undone the barrel nuts and could lift the barrels slightly by turning the engine over, but the pistons remained stuck despite regular gentle persuasion from the hide hammer. I needed to up the game, so made up a couple of alloy billets and put these on top of the pistons. I then took an old open-ended spanner and some washers and by using two head bolts wound the spanner onto the alloy billets to put some pressure onto the pistons. I also added some Coca-Cola to the mix in the bores to give

The seized pistons were well and truly stuck. Here the spanner is bearing down on a pair of alloy blocks with pressure being applied from the two head bolts.

it a bit more ommph! Then I left it alone for a few days to let the pressure and the Coke work its magic.

After the heavy-duty stripping, I wanted to get the speedometer and tachometer off for refurbishment: this would get them out of the way, since if any outside work is involved it is always better to get the work done sooner rather than later. The bike came with a pair of original and correct Smiths instruments, complete with the Norton 'green globe' logo, still mounted on the top yoke. Each clock was held in its pod with two small nuts that were just balls of rust. With lots of penetrating oil and a bit of gentle persuasion the nuts came off without ripping the studs out of the cases. Getting the clocks out of the alloy pods was a bit more of a challenge as the steel clock studs were corroded solidly into the alloy of the pods. More penetrating oil, and gentle easing and levering around the studs, eventually got the clocks to move out of the pods. The rev counter was in

pretty good condition, all in one piece, but with some marks on the dial. The speedo was worse, with a rusted bezel and a cracked glass, and its dial was not in as good condition as that on the tachometer. Both instruments' needles responded to a twiddle with a screwdriver in the drive, but as they had been static for a long time all the grease would have dried out. Even if they did work properly when refitted, they would fail very quickly in normal use. The alloy pods had a fair bit of corrosion, but no deep pitting. A quick go at one with some fine wet and dry took off the corrosion, so I put them in the 'alloy polishing' box, for future treatment.

The second 'outside' service I would use was chroming. The main parts on the 1971 Commando that were chromed as standard were the footrest hangers, brake pedal, headlamp brackets and chainguard (ignoring the wheel rims, which I would replace with new alloy items, and the exhaust, which was missing anyway). My chainguard looked to be beyond chroming, so was added to the list of replacement items; indeed the rest of the items that had come with the bike were all pretty rusty and beyond a lick of solvol. These were delivered to PJS Polishing, a local polishing company run by a relative, to get them polished up and chromed. The owner inspected the parts and reckoned that they should come up well, but pointed out that the inner edge of the headlamp brackets may not take the plating too well and may need painting after chroming.

After all this dismantling I decided that I wanted to get something finished, so the next job was to clean up and repaint the battery carrier and air cleaner assembly. The front plate came up well: it had a small amount of pitting and I sprayed it with silver Smoothite from an aerosol can. Then the rear plate was unbolted from the battery carrier and wire brushed to remove the rust and the occasional bit of paint. It was painted using black Smoothite. This gave a reasonable finish, but both parts were quite badly pitted with rust and probably needed a proper respray using primer/filler for a perfect finish. However they will not be visible in normal use and the Smoothite will kill the rust, so the less than perfect finish will do. Once the paint had cured, I bolted the back plate onto the battery carrier with new stainless bolts and washers and with a new air cleaner gauze and element. I assembled the complete air cleaner assembly and it actually looked quite good.

The next job was to get the powertrain out of the frame and send the frame off to be blasted and powder coated. When I bought the bike, however, the head was off and it definitely needed some attention. I had bought a set of stainless acorn nuts for the rocker covers from eBay: while they brightened up the somewhat corroded unit, they reminded me that the exhaust retaining locknuts were firmly fixed in the head, complete with the cut-off remains of the exhaust pipes. I had been dosing the locknuts with penetrating oil and I set about undoing them when my special exhaust-releasing 'C' spanner arrived. Of course they were solid and did not move, and with the head off it was impossible to get any real leverage. So the head was bolted back onto the bike and the spe-

cial tool applied onto the locknuts and hand pressure applied, followed by full body weight. When this had no effect I elected to apply some shock treatment with assistance from a hammer. The left-hand side locknut reluctantly succumbed to the treatment after a few enthusiastic blows, and unscrewed to expose a set of pristine threads in the alloy head: this was a good outcome as folklore (and experience) had it that Commando head threads were invariably butchered and always need expensive surgery to fix them. Turning to the other side, it had not shifted even after a concentrated spell of increasingly brutal hammering. So it was out with the blowtorch to heat up the head and the nut, but the nut remained stubbornly fixed. I applied more heat, more penetrating oil and a good half can of WD40, and then started on the ring with a drift and hammer. After a while the nut reluctantly started to turn and following a couple of revolutions I could wind it off by hand with the 'C' spanner. I was surprised to see that these threads were also fine, so I made a mental note to use lots of copper grease on reassembly, and new nuts and locking rings were placed on the 'to order' list. I could now remove the head and prepare to get the powertrain out of the frame.

The Commando suspends its powertrain and its swinging arm from two rubber-bushed Isolastic mountings. This means that, while it seems that all you need to do is take out two long bolts to get the complete powertrain and rear suspension out (forgetting the head steady, but the bike's head was off anyway), the job was a bit more complicated than that. According to the manual you could get the engine and gearbox out simply by removing the primary drive, taking out the rear Isolastic retaining stud and unbolting the front Isolastic unit from the frame. So, the first job was to take off the primary drive. I'd already taken off the primary chain case outer cover, and the alternator stator was the next thing to go, followed by the rotor – with the seized engine I could undo the rotor nut easily with no need to lock the primary drive and my universal puller made short work of pulling the rotor off the shaft. The clutch was next on the list and, using the approved tool to compress the diaphragm spring, I was able to remove the diaphragm spring (there are dire warnings about trying to remover the spring and its retaining circlip and I could see that it would be a foolish person who attempts this job without the proper tool) and I could undo the clutch centre nut with the Norvil clutch locking tool. With the help of the Norvil engine sprocket puller the whole primary drive came off in one piece without a struggle. I cannot recommend too stronly buying, begging, borrowing or stealing the right special tools as they turn tricky jobs into a doddle. A good tip I discovered the hard way is to use cable ties to keep together parts such as the clutch and all its various nuts and spacers in the order they fell off the bike before you consign them to the 'these bits are OK, so just need a quick clean before reassembly' box, since memory just doesn't work after a couple of months and parts books could be wrong. A brief inspection of the parts did not turn up any unexpected problems apart from some grotty looking friction plates, which would be replaced on rebuilding. Three nuts hold the inner chain case onto the engine and, with their locking tabs knocked flat, they came out without difficulty and I was ready to get the engine out. That's where things started to get tricky. The front Isolastic mount was fixed to the crankcases with two bolts and to the frame with one big bolt. The frame bolt was corroded solidly in place. Apparently this was not uncommon: looking at the state of the mount it had obviously had more than its fair share of road dirt and water sprayed on it. The manual says to move the bolt head so it misses the timing cover, then drive it out. The bolt moved round but would not drive out as it was firmly fixed to the Isolastic spacer tube inside the mount. I cut off the rubber boots and added loads of WD40 and penetrating oil, which of course had no effect, so it was out with the blowtorch, but the bolt remained struck. Stepping back and taking a long hard look at the bike, I realized that if I took out the gearbox and its mounting plates with the swinging arm, and if I unbolted the engine from the front Isolastic mount (two bolts), I could shift the engine back

and lift it out, leaving the Isolastic mount in place in the frame.

In order to take out the gearbox and swinging arm I had to remove the rear shock absorbers. While I was down that end of the bike I took off the rear brake drum and sprocket as well. The hub nut that held this on had been put on by a large gorilla and needed an awful lot of leverage applied to it to get it off. Incidentally the special rear unit top mounting bolts, which carry the alloy discs (missing) that hold the seat on, were impressively rusty and close examination of the rear suspension units showed that the springs and damper rods were shot, with peeling chrome, so there were a couple of extras to add to the new parts list.

The rear Isolastic mounting was in good condition and uncorroded, and its frame fixing stud pulled out by hand. The complete gearbox, engine plates and swinging arm assembly could then be unbolted from the back of the engine and moved backwards, giving me enough room to pull the engine back from the front mount and lift it out of the frame. The gearbox and swinging arm assembly could then be wiggled out of the frame. With the engine out of the way I could get a socket on the head of the front Isolatic mounting bolt, but it still did not want to move. So I took a hacksaw and, working between the tube cup and the collar on the timing (bolt head) side, I cut through the bolt and Isolastic tube, making sure I avoided the frame lug and the Isolastic mount. Then I could take out the somewhat shortened bolt head and, with a bit of wiggling, took the front mount off of the frame with the remains of the centre bolt still in place. The Isolastics, with the remains of the bolt still in place, were pushed out relatively easily and the front mount was ready for the blasters and powder coaters.

With the gearbox cradle I pushed out the upper Isolastics by hand; after undoing the two big bolts that fix the gearbox in position I was able, with a bit of thought, to liberate the gearbox from its cradle. It was a bit like a 3-D puzzles – the box obviously got in between the two plates, I just had to work out how to get it out. The

Mike at MSC with the newly powder-coated frame, swinging arm, gearbox cradle oil tank and front engine mount.

swinging arm spindle pushed out easily, still with all its fittings, and had no apparent play but was full of grease rather than oil – the disadvantage of fitting a grease nipple to a fitting that needs oiling. So the cradle and the swinging arm joined the frame and the front mount in the 'blasting and powder coating' pile.

One thing on the frame that I had noticed while grovelling about dismantling the primary drive was a brazed-on lug behind the side stand post. With the frame devoid of all the other bits of bike, I could now see it clearly: it was a clamp for a bolt-on side stand. I vaguely remembered reading something about the Commando side stand and its propensity for falling off, and the 1971 parts manual showed the stand being held onto its post by a circlip. The Norvil and RGM catalogues did not list any of the 1971 parts, so I spoke to Les Emery at Norvil, who pointed out that the pin-type side stand fitting was dangerous as the side stand invariably fell off and went into the rear wheel – with potentially fatal consequences. For this reason he did not stock the stand and associated clip. Norton (and Norvil) do a conversion kit that can be welded onto the frame and uses the later (1972 on) side stand. As mine had a bracket already fixed in place, I tried a bolt-on side stand I just happened to have lying around in the garage, and the bolt centres lined up. That was good news and a close inspection of the frame did not show any further problems. I had already taken off all the bolts and other fixings on the frame, apart from a very rusty Dzus fastener on the drive side that was used to fix on the side panel. This came off with a bit of persuasion and the frame was ready for its trip to the powder coaters. The final job on the frame was to carefully remove the VIN plate. This required me to cut off the heads of the four brass rivets and prise off the plate.

With the engine on the bench it was obvious that it needed a really good clean and a bit of further investigation as to how to release the pistons: the pressure, oil and Coke had not worked so I needed a new approach. The gearbox had one minor problem – it did not seem to have any gears in it. I could turn the drive sprocket and the

mainshaft, but the two seemed to have no relationship, as if the box was in neutral. I could waggle the gear lever up and down until the cows come home, but gears there were none – apart from neutral.

Rolling Chassis

With the frame and other bits and pieces taken to the powder coaters, the next job was to recondition the forks and yokes. The yokes just needed a good wire brushing and a coat of silver Smoothite. They had some surface pitting from the rust but look alright. The old steering lock was driven out: unlike Triumph items there was no grub screw to hold it in, it was just a tight fit in the top yoke. Norvil do a 'fork kit' that covers all the wearing items (bushes, gaskets and seals) and I also ordered stanchions, stainless steel bottom yoke nut, washer, top nuts and new yoke Allen bolts, handlebar clamps with bolts and gaiters (the short ones, since I do like exposed chrome stanchions on a bike), and a new steering lock finished off the order.

I had already separated the legs from the yokes and taken off the top nuts to remove the instrument pods, so the first job was to disassemble each leg. This meant unscrewing the steel top ring that resided under the gaiters I had already removed. Both legs came apart with no problems; the top rings were stiff, but a strap wrench eventually got them unscrewed, and then it was just a case of pulling up on the stanchion to drive out the seal and top bush. Next I had to undo the nut in the base of the fork leg to get the damper rod and spring, and the job was done.

With the forks in pieces most of the bits looked to be in pretty good condition, but the old stanchions were badly worn in places and the bushes were all a bit worn. I did not strip down the damper rod and spring, just gave them a clean, and cleaned out the sludge from the bottom of each alloy slider. That's one really nice thing about the Commando – there's lots of good quality alloy that polishes up a treat! The fork sliders were no exception. I scraped off the old Missouri safety sticker and used some 800 grade

The bike starts to go back together. Here the refurbished battery cradle is fitted, along with the oil tank and air filter assembly.

wet and dry to clean up each slider. Then I polished them up using a mop kit in the electric drill. The reassembly was trouble-free and I used the old top bushes to drive in the new seals with the stanchion already in place. This was a lot easier to do than on Triumph or BSA forks, which have their seals in the chromed seal holders and are the devil to install without the correct tool. The new gaiters needed to be softened up in hot water and have some silicon grease sprayed on them before they would slot into place.

With both fork legs completed I gave the instrument pods a polish up, again starting with 800 wet and dry and then finishing them off with the polishing mop. All in all the refurbishment went well, without problems and using good quality replacement parts that all fitted.

The frame had needed three coats of powder coating to cover most of the rust pitting and the finish was really good, with a lovely deep black gloss. The downside was that it was necessary to file the paint out from inside most of the holes in the frame in order to get the bolts through! The swinging arm, engine plates and front Isolastic mountings did not need so much work, and building up the rolling chassis was now possible. Re-riveting the VIN plate onto the headstock

The frame was now ready to have the forks and wheels fitted. Note the VIN plate reattached to the headstock, and the yokes ready for the fork legs.

using new brass rivets was the first job, followed by refitting the rear engine plates/gearbox carrier/swinging arm pivot. New Mark 3 type Isolastics with the 'vernier' type adjusters were fitted using lots of red rubber grease, and the swinging arm was fitted with a new pin, bushes and 'O' rings. Luckily the spindle mounting in the plates was tight in the cradle so an oversized pin was not needed. I reused the end caps and its thin retaining spindle, and spent some time unsuccessfully trying to keep the oil in the bearing while putting the end plates back on. Eventually I took out the nut in the middle of the swinging arm pivot and pumped oil in from there, which seemed to work.

With the engine plate/Isolastic/swinging arm assembly built up, it could be fitted to the bike. This was achieved with some grunting and groaning and some removal of powder coating between the mounting lugs. Now I had the top Isolastic bolted in, I could fit the previously renovated battery carrier and the oil tank, and with new rear suspension units fitted using stainless bolts, new 'Knurled Knobs' for the seat and polished up 'Z' plates, the project was actually beginning to look like a bike.

Next up it was the wheels and the brakes. The rear brake came apart easily and with little rust. With new shoes, a good clean-up and a new twin row bearing it was ready to refit. The front brake was a bit of a disaster. It had suffered from rust and was a right royal pain to dismantle. I had decided to buy a stiffening kit, basically comprising new expanders and pivots, with a great big plate bolted to them to prevent any flex from the brake plate. These were fitted as standard to the last TLS brakes. The pivots were well and truly corroded in place in the plate, and it took serious surgery to get the lower one out. After heat and brute force failed, I had to drill the pivot out in the lath, and then cut through the thin tube of steel left in the alloy plate and pick it out – not easy and I was worried that I would destroy the brake plate. All the brake's internals had seen better days and needed replacing. The screws holding in the air intake and exit grills were thoroughly corroded in place and I could only get them out by using heat followed by

chiselling them round – even so half of the exit shield ones broke off. New grills were needed, as were new springs, operating arms and tie rod. The only original parts were the brake plate itself and the two pivot bushes. One last job on the front brake was to put a 45-degree chamfer on the leading edge of each shoe, which should make the brake more progressive and cut down any tendency to grab. On top of all this, the hub was badly corroded and needed a good skim: when I finally got the bike on the road I found that the drum was too far gone and had to buy a new one.

After all this grief the wheel building was easy. Sitting in the garden in the sun, with both hubs cleaned up and polished, the brand new stainless spokes and Akront flanged alloy rims were laced on and, as usual with Central Wheel Components rims and spokes, no problems emerged. I had taken photos of the wheels before I dismantled them, and checked the offset from the originals (front 4mm to the rim from the brake hub face, and rear 6mm to the rim from the cush drive side), so truing up was easy.

The next task was to put together the rolling chassis. This is always a significant stage in a restoration as it means you actually have something that is a functioning bicycle, albeit not a motor bicycle!

I ordered up a pair of tyres. There are a reasonable set of options for Commandos on 19in rims, with the 4.10 × 19 Dunlop TT100 vying with various offerings from Avon, including Roadriders and Roadrunners. I chose TT100s, for no reasons other than that I like the feel of them on my Bonneville, they've never given me any 'moments' in the dry or wet, contemporary road tests rated them and I like the look of them! Fitting the new covers with new tubes and rim tapes was reasonably easy with lots of washing-up liquid. I know you're not supposed to use it because it will rust the wheels, but with alloy rims, brass nipples and stainless spokes there was not a lot to rust. Anyway, I know its not such a good idea to leave the stuff on the tyres, so once I had checked that the air couldn't get out, I let the tyres down and gave them a good hose down to rinse out the washing-up liquid.

The rolling chassis, now complete with new stainless steel mudguards. This is always a significant point in a restoration as you can see progress is being made.

It was at this point that I realized that I needed to refit the rear hub's alloy cover, but I had to get out the remains of the screws that fix it in place. I had chiselled the heads off to get the cover off initially, and now had six stubs to attack. They still did not want to budge, so I chiselled them flat and drilled a fresh set of 2mm holes to one side for the new fixing screws – amazingly without breaking the drill bit! Then I found that the new screws would only go in about halfway before they became very tight. I experimented on an old bit of alloy with a 2.5mm drill and found that the screws were a bit too loose, which was why I used a 2mm drill to start with. So I redrilled the first half of each 2mm hole to 2.5mm and this worked, with the screws fitting snugly and holding the cover in place. Before I fitted the cover, I gave the clean alloy interior of the hub a coating of ACF50 to prevent corrosion: I also applied some down the screw holes in the hope of making it possible to remove the screws at a later date.

So that was the wheels all done and dusted.

Pete the polisher had some bad news regarding the headlamp 'ears' or brackets, as they were too far gone to be chromed, so I had to order a new pair. The arrival of the brackets meant I could fit the yokes (or triple tree as the Americans like to call them) to the frame. Before the bottom yoke was fully tightened up, I inserted the rubber 'O' rings that cushion the brackets between the yokes – two at the bottom and one at the top – and used Vaseline to keep them in place while I positioned the brackets. Then I could push the rebuilt fork leg up into the yokes. By tightening the lower pinch bolt I fixed the leg in place. Filling each fork leg with the requisite 150cc of fork oil took a bit of time and required the slider to be gently moved up and down to get the oil past the spring and damper: warming the oil helped to speed up the process. Then I could push up the fork slider relative to the stanchion, which lifted the spring and damper out of the top of the fork and enabled me to screw the top nut onto the fork damper rod. Then I let the slider slide down and was able to refix the top nut with the instrument pod attached. Then it was time to torque up the top nuts and bottom yoke nut to 30ft lb and the job was completed without drama or special tools, whereas BSA and Triumph forks, with their external springs, require a special puller to insert the leg into the yokes.

I had also ordered new stainless mudguards from RGM before doing the forks. Fixing the front mudguard bridge to the sliders was by two bolts each side and, with the rear stay fixed to the fork sliders and the mudguard, I could fit the front wheel and brake.

When I ordered the brackets, I had also ordered a 7in chrome headlamp shell, rim and the light switch and warning lights from Norvil. These were fitted next, giving a complete front end, apart from the handlebars, switches and the headlamp wiring.

The footrests were the next to receive attention. The footrest hangers and rear brake pedal had come back from the chromers and looked superb. The timing side one, with its integral footrest bolted straight on to the 'Z' plate, just needed the rubber to finish it off. The drive side had to have the brake pedal fixed on using the nifty little Norton grease nipple, which was extended to fit into a groove on the pedal pivot and fixes the pedal in place. A Norvil pedal spring was fitted, which was important as it prevents the pedal swinging down and hitting the road if the rear brake cable fails. A new stainless steel brake pedal stop bolt and nut were fitted to the brake adjuster, and a new stop light micro-switch from Vehicle Wiring Products was bolted to the plate on the hanger. With the assembly complete it was bolted to the 'Z' plate.

According to the parts manual, the rear mudguard was fixed at three points: two bolts fix the lower front to the rear of the battery carrier, a plate that bolts to the frame plate at the rear of the main spine provides a second fixing, and a semicircular clip fixes the guard to the rear of the seat loop. This was very straightforward and easy to sort while the rear wheel was out. It's also a good idea to fix the horn in its position below the battery carrier before fixing on the rear guard. With the guard fixed in place the rear wheel was persuaded into place. The new cush drive rubbers proved an effective obstacle to fitting, but the wheel was eventually levered into place and the spindle and spacer fitted, to give me a rolling chassis. There was one more job to do: fitting the handlebars so I could actually wheel the thing around. Four Allen bolts – easy … until I tried to wind the bolts tight and they all started to stiffen up after about five turns. The threads in the top yoke were alright but needed a good clean out, so I ran a tap down them all – and lots of rusty crud came out of each.

Engine

The next challenge was to strip down and rebuild the seized engine. First off was the points and advance retard unit. The points and back plate were in poor condition and the a/r unit was seized solid. The timing cover was next and its screws were suspiciously loose. But with the cover off there were no unpleasant surprises. It was clean, everything that was supposed to be there was present and there was no evidence of any bodging. The oil pump nuts were very tight, but the pump came off easily after using the dodge of turning it so it wound off the drive worm, the spiral drive gear was wound off the end of the crank (clockwise – it's a left-hand thread as the manual usefully informs you) and the drive pinion came off in my hand. The nut holding on the camshaft sprocket was tight, and the manual tells you not to apply brute force with a hammer. Fortunately it succumbed to a socket and I used Norvil's special legs on their engine sprocket puller to pull the sprocket off its taper with the timing chain and intermediate sprocket still attached. Finally I removed the camshaft drive chain tensioner. All the nuts, washers, spacers and other bits and bobs were bound together using cable ties in the order they came off.

So, with the timing side stripped, the big issue could no longer be avoided. As the pistons were still firmly seized, how could I split the cases? If I could split the cases then I could get at the bottom of the pistons and try more exotic de-seizing stuff from the other end while the crank and cases were being refurbished. I knew that the crank was not seized as I could move the barrels up and down a little. Although the barrels were spigotted into the cases and held on with studs, I reckoned that if I could remove the studs then I should be able to split the cases with the barrels still attached to the pistons. With all the studs wound out of the cases this looked feasible. There were three studs and two set screws holding the cases together, and the big nut behind the barrels was seized and inaccessible, so it had to be chiselled off. The cases parted with a bit of gentle rubber malletting, and finally the crank was free with the con rods, pistons and barrels still attached. The cases looked to be in good nick, but there was a fair amount of black sludge in them. There was a good deal of silicone gasket material floating around the cases, with long strings of it all over the place. This was not a good sign as it meant the engine had been got at. The big ends were accessible and swiftly removed, and the crank and rod/barrel assembly were separated. The big ends were shot: there was a dull grey appearance on the shells and copper showing on one. On one rod the shells were in the wrong way round, with the hole in the shell in the cap, not in the rod. This was possibly why the piston(s) were seized, as oil was supposed to flow from the big end through the hole in the shell to a drilling in the con rod and then spray out to the barrel wall. The crank journals were scored as well, so the crank needed a regrind.

I took the bare crankcases, timing cover and the primary chain case over to Motor Sport Coatings to be aqua-blasted. A couple of days later I was able to pick them up at the same time I collected the frame and other bits I had put in for powder coating. The results were impressive. They were also able to repair a crack in the outer chain case where a footrest must have come into contact with it. The timing case and chain case were quite heavily corroded, and I would need to break out the wet and dry to smooth them down before getting them onto the polishing mop.

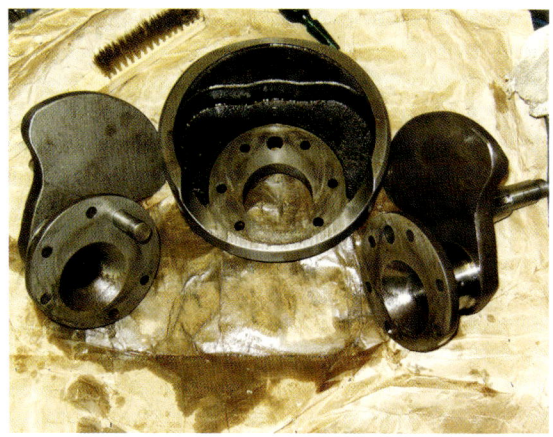

The Commando crank in pieces, ready for reassembly. Note the hollow big end journals: these voids form the sludge trap.

Before I could start the rebuild I had to sort out the stuck pistons. First I taped cardboard to the rods to protect them from the barrels, and then dosed the underside of the pistons with WD40 and penetrating oil. Both pistons were seized: I had been hoping that one would be free, so that was a disappointment. But at least I could now have a go at both ends of the pistons. My priority was to save the con rods and barrels. One side eventually succumbed to heat and brute force, but the other was obviously made of sterner stuff and even an hour in the oven at 250°C made no difference to it.

As recounted previously, the crank's big end journals were scored and these were farmed out to Roe Engineering in Fleet for the regrind, along with a copy of the relevant page from the workshop manual showing the radius needed between the edge of the journal and rest of the crank, -0.090in. Failure to correctly grind this radius will result in the crank failing. Along with the crank I took in the barrels with the recalcitrant piston still firmly in place to see if they could do anything with their 20 ton press.

And two weeks later, I had a phone call saying it was all done. I whizzed down there to find a reground crank -0.010in at the first regrind, again implying the mileage was correct) and the barrels separated from the piston and rod. It had taken eight tons to shift the piston, along with some drilling of the piston crown, but the con rod and barrels had survived. The barrels had been very badly corroded, and clouds of red rust dust were generated as Roe Engineering slowly cut into the corrosion, until eventually they hit sound metal. The rebore took the barrels out to +.060 thou, the maximum size that pistons were available. There were still some slight marks on the bores but it was to be hoped that they would be alright.

Now I could get on with rebuilding the bottom end of the engine. Norvil produce a 'bottom end rebuild kit' that contains everything that I needed, including main bearings, big end shells, crank and con rod nuts and bolts, and other assorted odds and sods. So I ordered up the kit with the right sized shells, and then set to reassembling the crankshaft. New Emgo +060 thou pistons and rings came from eBay.

The Commando crank is made up of three components: two cheeks carrying a big end each, bolted to a central flywheel. Before I started to put the crank back together, I was puzzled by its construction. The two journals bolted to the central flywheel, and on my 750 were fixed by a single dowel, four bolts and two studs. The kit supplied from Andover Norton via Norvil comprised six studs, as the later 750cc/850cc parts book also stated. So that was OK then, although the International Norton Owners Association Tech Digest points out that this change was made for cost reasons, since studs are cheaper than bolts. The Tech Digest also disclosed that the crankcase nuts and studs should be replaced with those used on the post-200,000 numbered engines as they were a better fit and unlikely to loosen off. I was still wondering how the dowel was retained in place, as the locating holes in the crank cheeks were drilled right through, but then realized that the nut retaining plate covered the hole, and so stopped the dowel from flying out as well as stopping the nuts undoing. With the various bits of crank laid out on the bench, reassembly could commence. The first issue was that I had not marked up the flywheel to say which side was which, but luckily the

photo I had taken earlier showed some marks, from which I could determine the correct side. Putting the crank cheeks onto the flywheel was reasonably simple, but working out which studs went where was the second part of the puzzle: there were two long ones and two short ones, and eight long nuts and four short nuts. Obviously the long nuts went with the short studs, and the parts manual showed the four similar-sized short studs went on the 'top' and 'bottom' of the crank with the long two at the three and nine o'clock positions. The final bit of the puzzle was to make sure the bottom two studs (the ones that were next to the locating dowel) were in place in the flywheel before locating the crank cheeks. You cannot fit them with the cheeks in place as they are too long: of course I found this out as I was loosely assembling the assembly, so I ended up with two dry runs. Finding out what torque setting to tighten the nuts to was a tad tricky: the official Norton workshop manual says to 'make sure they are very, very tight', useful advice but not very precise. The 750 manual for 1970 onwards says 35ft/lb (4.84kg/m) but that uses bolts as well as studs, the INOA Tech Digest says 25ft/lb (3.45kg/m) for studs and the Mark 3 manual says 30ft/lb (4.15kg/m), but this uses different studs, so I was a bit stumped as to what setting to use. Les Emery on the Norvil helpline

The Commando crank assembled. The central flywheel is sandwiched between the two outer shafts with their big end journals. The whole assembly is doweled and held together with studs and nuts.

recommended that I use 25ft/lb, stated in the INOA advice. The nuts on the bottom studs are shielded by the crank cheeks so you could not get a torque wrench on them anyway, so they were bolted together very tightly and locked in place with the tab washer.

With the crank back in one piece it was time to attach the connecting rods. First thing was to polish out the various nicks and scratches on the surface of both rods, then fit the new bolts. In the Norton Owners Club Commando Service Notes, John Hudson comments that the heads of the con rod bolts had a sharp edge and this could scrape a shaving of Dural off the rod, preventing the bolt from being tightened down properly. Both my rods showed this 'feature' when I removed the old bolts. With the edges of the new bolts carefully polished, I fitted new big end bearings and then the rods to the crank. There was only one problem: one con rod nut decided not to cooperate and the socket could not grip it properly, so I could not torque it down to the 25ft/lb (3.45kg/m) required. Taking the nut off showed it had been rounded, so I had to order a new set of nuts.

With the crank finally assembled the crankcases needed to be prepped. Removing the old main bearings meant popping the cases in the oven for a quick thirty minutes at 150°C. The timing side dropped out without a problem, but the drive side outer had to be levered up micron by micron using a screwdriver since the casing prevented access from the outside. Then I had to clean them up after the aqua-blasting, wiping all the oil ways and stud holes to make sure that all of the blasting media was removed. The oil ways were cleaned using that old stalwart of the restorer, a pipe cleaner, to loosen everything and then blasting WD40 through the drillings until the WD40 came out clean – and it took a fair bit of blasting, pipe cleaning and blasting again. There was plenty of blast residue in the cylinder stud holes – remember I had to take the studs out to get the barrel off with the seized pistons – and there was some trapped behind the old main bearing outers that I had left in the cases.

The new superblend main bearings spent thirty minutes in the freezer, and then were dropped

The crank with connecting rods attached assembled into the crankcases. These have been aqua-blasted and then thoroughly cleaned to remove any trace of the blasting medium.

straight into the clean and rewarmed cases with a spot of Loctite to make sure they stayed there. The inner races fitted snugly onto the crank after being warmed in the oven and the cases were ready to come together for a trial fit. The book says 0.005–0.015in of end float is permissible, so I popped a 3 thou shim behind the drive side inner race on the crank and prayed – there was about 0.005–0.007in present when the cases were tightened. So I split the cases, put a thin smear of blue Hylomar on the case faces, fitted the camshaft into the drive side with its breather disc and spring, then put the cases back together and rechecked the end float and that the camshaft was spinning freely.

With the cases back together, I almost decided to pop on the resprayed barrels and shiny new pistons, but luckily I remembered that I should rebuild the timing side first, because I needed to lock up the engine to torque up the main pinion nut and the camshaft nut, and could not do that easily with the barrels on.

I inspected the oil pump and while it felt a bit rough as I turned it over, as if there was some foreign matter in there, it had no end float on the drive gear so the body was not worn. I gave it a thorough clean out by flushing WD40 and then thin oil through it. At first the output of both sides was decidedly murky – obviously clean oil was a long forgotten memory for the motor! However the pump action grew smoother as flushing continued, and eventually I had a smooth running pump that returned good clean oil. As there was still no end float, it was fit to go back in the motor. Carefully reassembling the timing side components was simple, but making sure that the holes in the new oil pump gasket lined up was important, as was making sure the cam timing was right, especially as I was fitting a new cam chain. With the oil pump nuts torqued up and the cam chain tensioner installed, I tightened up the oil pump drive (left-hand thread) and the camshaft nut (right-hand thread, with some Loctite on it as well), while locking the crankshaft with a rod through the small ends.

The barrels were next, using plenty of graphite grease on the cams and followers, refitting the barrel studs and then fitting the new pistons to the con rods, making sure the new circlips were firmly embedded in their grooves. The ring gaps were checked (about 0.012 thou of an inch) in

Fitting the barrels to the engine with ring compressors.

the barrel and the rings were placed on the pistons, and the ring compressors were fitted. With the pistons supported on a brass rod and loads of grease and oil, the barrels were gently slid over the rings and bolted down.

Finally the timing cover had new seals fixed on the oil feed, contact breaker hole and oil pump. With its new gasket in place the cover was screwed in position with a new set of Allen screws. So was the engine sorted and ready to fit into the frame.

Gearbox

Next up was the gearbox. Once it was out of the bike it was apparent that it was in neutral, since the gearbox sprocket and the mainshaft could be rotated independently, and moving the gear lever had no effect on this state whatsoever. So this was not going to be a 'sling it back in the frame and it'll be fine' scenario. I cleaned the muck off the outer cases with Jizer and set to. The cases were in good nick, and the outer cover screws came out with a bit of help on a couple from my impact driver, apart from one buried deep in the casing by the gear lever. This one was a bit chewed up and just a tad too deep to get at with the impact driver – the head of the driver was too wide to go into the hole in the casing and the bit was too short. Rather than persist and ruin the head of the screw, I bought a slim 8mm socket that cleared the sides of the hole when on the impact driver bit, and so I was able to use the impact driver to drive the socket to drive the bit to batter the screw round until it came out. All the screws were the original slotted head items and will be replaced with Allen screws.

With the outer cover off there was a lot more water than oil sloshing about in the gearbox. The bike was still living up to its rather damp reputation, but the innards did not look too bad apart from the rather nasty brown residue of oil, water, bits of old gasket, gasket goo and general muck. It was time to whip off the inner cover, which was held on by seven nuts that came off easily. Inside it was not as bad as I had feared – in fact it was pretty good. The lack of gears was due to the camplate plunger being seized, preventing the plate from rotating. I was going to replace the bearings in the case and had bought the 'short AMC gearbox kit' from Norvil, which included these bearings, so I was not too concerned that the originals felt rough. A tip I picked up was to heat up the case from the back with a blowtorch before pulling out the layshaft. This releases the layshaft bearing from the case and it comes out easily still attached to the layshaft, where it could be removed at leisure.

With all the gubbins out, I could inspect the internals. Apart from the bearings, all were in good nick: the gear teeth showed some surface rust, which cleaned with WD40, but none of the teeth showed any pitting or other evidence of the hardening wearing through. Bushes were a good fit on the shafts, and the dogs on the gears were unworn. The camplate was fine, and even the selector forks were alright. So it was just clean everything up and, in the immortal Haynes Manual words, 'reassembly is the reverse of disassembly'.

First off, after soaking in penetrating oil overnight, the seized camplate plunger came out of the body with a spot of tapping and gentle persuasion. The design helped: there is a tiny drilling in the top of the plunger that prevents a hydraulic lock and this let the penetrating oil into the assembly. The unit must have had some water in it since when I picked it up the spring fell into two parts due to corrosion. So another item was added to the order list.

Replacing the gearbox bearings should have been easy. I had taken the old bearings out of the shell and inner casing, and cleaned up the outsides. I then heated up the inner case and main shell in the oven to about 180°C, and somewhat belatedly put the new bearings in the freezer. I learned three important lessons while trying to put the mainshaft (sleeve gear) bearing in: Loctite goes off quite quickly when hot, a few minutes in the freezer doesn't shrink the bearing that much, and bashing the outer edge of a bearing with a drift could result in a bit of slippage, a dented cage and a wait while Norvil send a new bearing. It was my fault – like an idiot I did not use the purpose-made drift to get the new bear-

The gearbox semi-assembled, with the mainshaft at the top, above the layshaft, selector forks in place and the camplate to the right. The forked arm at the top right connects to the gear change mechanism.

ing in (actually the old bearing). The other two bearings dropped in place with no problems and I then spent some time polishing up the outer cover.

One thing that was not shown in any of the workshop manuals or the parts book was the positioning of the layshaft fourth gear – the one on the casing end of the layshaft, next to the bearing. This gear had a raised centre on one face, and this should face the bearing. I only found this out while reading an old copy of Classic Mechanics, and luckily this was before I started the rebuild.

With the new mainshaft bearing in place in the shell, it was time to put the rest of the box back together. Following the workshop manual, I put the gear change quadrant in, initially placing it as high up as it would go (the manual says 'until the top quadrant radius was in line with the top front cover stud'). I realized it was too high when I had put in the camplate and found that the end cover would not go on with the quadrant all the way up. Moving it down a tad, in accordance with the manual, made sense and then it did not foul the joint. It emphasizes an important lesson I've learned from doing gearboxes: always stop after each operation and take a look at what you've done. Another couple of gems when working with gearboxes are:

Everything should turn or rotate easily. If a shaft locks up then the gears are on wrong – especially if it all locks up when you are tightening up a cover.

Don't force anything – if something doesn't fit where or how you want it to fit, then you are wrong.

In both cases just step back and check.

New rubber seals went on the camplate and quadrant shafts. I popped the camplate plunger in place with a new spring and a touch of Loctite on its threads to seal it. I also put a blob of grease on the bottom of the plunger spring in the hope of protecting it against any condensation, as it sits at the lower end of the box.

Having built up the mainshaft, layshaft and selector forks in the shell, I screwed in the selector fork rod, again with a touch of Loctite to seal the thread. When I fitted the inner cover, tightening it down caused the box to seize up. So it was off with the cover and check that the shafts were properly located in their bearings and that the gears were all in the right position: I'd put the mainshaft first gear in the wrong way round. With that cog reversed, the inner cover went back on properly and I fitted a new mainshaft oil seal, spacer and the original, good condition 19-tooth drive sprocket along with a new lock washer and locating screw. In the inner cover I fitted the nut on the other end of the main shaft, adding some Loctite. It was time to sort out the outer cover. I fitted new 'O' rings to the gear change and kickstart shafts. I tried to fit the outer cover but it would not go on. After dismantling the change mechanism and general fiddling around, I eventually found that the two dowels on the case were stopping it from locating. I only discovered this by taking the dowels out of the inner case and realigned them before carefully locating the outer case on one and manoeuvring the case around to line up the second – at which point it went on and I realized I'd left off the gasket. It also pays to make sure that part of the clutch operating mechanism is not fouling the inner case as well. Once the outer cover was on, it was time to check that I had all the gears in place by operating the gear change mechanism while rotating the final drive sprocket and mainshaft – and that there were four gears and one neutral, just as the manual says. Finally with the outer cover on (with its gasket) I could fit the gearbox into the frame.

This proved to be a bit interesting, due to Norton's gearbox fixing mechanism. The box had a big stud at the bottom, and it pivots on this to adjust the primary chain. The upper mount locates in a slot in the engine plates so it could move, and was locked in place by an adjuster comprising a screw thread that fits in a hole in a small block bolted to the engine plates. It sounds easy, but if you put the block in place before you put the gearbox in, the gearbox fouls the block's nut, so you have to put it in after fitting the gearbox and there is almost no space to get at the nut to tighten it up. I eventually managed to fit the block in place with a lot of fiddling. With the gearbox in place, I peered around the somewhat full garage and noticed the engine, sans head, ready to go into the frame. Needing some bench room, I lifted it over to the frame and dropped it in without any problems, apart from the bottom rear bolt needing some encouragement with the rubber mallet to clear the bottom frame rail. Otherwise all the bolts went in clean as a whistle and it was back in place within about 10 minutes: I was so surprised I took some pictures and went for a sit down and a cuppa!

Cylinder Head and Primary Drive

Next came the cylinder head. Although the head was off the bike when I bought it, it was complete if somewhat corroded and filthy, with the remains of both sparkplugs still in the holes. When I say remains I mean just that – the threaded part of both plugs was all that was there. Before I tackled the plugs, I needed to strip the head down. First I had to strip out the rocker spindles.

Engine and gearbox assembled in the cradle and frame. The Isolastics, top and front, are clearly visible.

The cylinder head was in a bit of a state. Note the remains of the spark plugs, the sawn-off exhaust pipes, and general rust and decay.

There are four of these, each one living behind the neat little covers on the side of the head. The covers were rusty, but I had already bought replacement ones and new bolts in stainless steel from the Netley Marsh Autojumble. I pulled the rocker spindles out of the head, using one of the old crank studs screwed into the spindle, and then winded them out using a nut on the stud and a socket as a spacer. This released the rockers and their spring washers, which gave access to the valve springs. The springs were removed with a Triumph valve spring compressor and the valves were driven out of the guides with my brass drift – they were very stiff, but did not seem to be corroded in place. A close inspection of the valves showed the stems and seats to be in pretty good condition, but I have never seen so much pitting on the surfaces of all of them (I could only imagine that they had been corroding gently for a long time), and they were replaced. The valve seats in the head actually looked alright. With most of the hardware out of the way, I put the head into the garage oven at 180°C to get some heat into it and help get the valve guides out: they are cheap and as I was going to have new valves, I might as well change them. The guides drifted out easily with some spirited hammering on my brass drift, and then with a bare head I could start on the stuck remains of the plugs. After a number of attempts to get them out using heat and other methods to try to turn the remains, I did what I should have done in the first place and took it down to Roe Engineering (who fixed the crank, released the stuck piston and did the rebore) and asked them to drill them out and helicoil them if needed. At a cost of £25 per side, Roe Engineering drilled out the offending ex-plugs and put in stainless helicoils.

With the remains of the plugs removed I could now start the refurbishing of the head. The new guides were put in the freezer over night (its well worth wrapping them in a couple of plastic bags and hiding them at the back, both to get them really cold), and then the head was cleaned with Jizer and put in the dishwasher for a good clean. After the cleaning the head went back in the oven for a thorough heating, and the new guides

were drifted in easily. With the guides in I could grind in the new valves, which went remarkably quick and easy and then I fitted the valves with their new springs – not forgetting the new heat insulating pads between the bottom cap and the head. While the head was still warm I drove the rocker spindles in, with the rockers and new thrust and Thackeray spring washers. Stainless steel end caps and bolts finished off the mechanical bits, and then I had to polish up the rocker covers, which were pretty rough. I started with really coarse 150 grade wet and dry just to get the corrosion off them. After working down the grades to 1200, and then using the buffing wheels, they came up quite well and matched the new stainless acorn nuts that fixed them in place. Before I put the head on I decided to fit the primary drive. The chain case needed a new felt washer for the main shaft seal behind the clutch. It was a bit a struggle to pick out the old one and then fit the new one, but it went in eventually. I bolted the inner chain case to the crankcases with a new gasket and three new bolts and tab washers, with a touch of Loctite stud sealer on the bolts as the holes are open to the crankcase. I could also check that the shims behind the case on the centre fixing bolt were correct – not too loose or too tight. Once the case was on, I realized I should have fitted the final drive chain while the sprocket was open to the air, but the new chain went on without too much of a struggle as there was still reasonable access even with the inner chain case in position. The engine sprocket, primary chain and clutch basket were fitted as a unit with a bit of jiggling of the gearbox position to get some slack on the primary chain. The use of cable ties to keep all the bits together made reassembly easy and the positioning of the spacers behind the clutch obvious. The alignment of the clutch and engine sprockets was checked as well to ensure they are in line. The clutch gained new friction plates and the muck of ages was cleaned off the drive plates with wet and dry paper. The clutch centre nut was torqued up to 70ft/lb and the clutch spring reinstated using the special tool. The Sparx alternator stator and rotor were fitted, with a new grommet for the output wires hopefully

Refurbished head fitted to the engine. New valves and springs and cleaned up rockers all help to make it look better. The large openings around the exhaust valves give good clearance for tappet adjustment.

Just behind the steering head is where the headlight loom, the two handlebar switch looms and the main loom meet – hence the spaghetti. Coils and front reflectors are mounted on their own bracket on the frame cross-member.

oil-proofed with some silicone sealant. With a new rubber sealing ring the polished primary chain case was bolted in place with a new stainless fixing bolt and washer.

Now it was time to refit the head. The manual shows how the pushrods needed to be positioned in the head with the inlet ones outboard, and then, when you drop the head in place, they would magically position themselves on the cam followers at the bottom of the barrel. To quote the Norton manual:

> Note that the pushrods could not do other than locate on the cam followers at the lower end.

Yeah, right, I thought: you do have to let the pushrods drop into the barrels, then fiddle them into position on the rockers after dropping the head onto the barrels. Once the head was resting loosely on the barrels, I fiddled each pushrod onto its rocker using a dentist's probe. Eventually

all four were in place and I just tweaked the outer four head bolts up so I could turn the engine over and check if all was operating as it should. And it was – all the tappets moved in turn, and there were no nasty clicks signifying that a pushrod was not properly positioned on the cam follower. It was not possible to tighten the head down using a torque wrench, due to the assortment of nuts and bolts and their positions, so I used my judgment to tighten them up, and the head was on.

At this point all the mechanical work was complete and the bike was rapidly approaching completion.

Wiring

The Commando's existing wiring harness had one big fault: the previous owner had cut it into several parts, presumably to remove it from the bike, and it was unusable. This was a bad thing from an originality aspect, but a good reason to

The Sparx combined regulator and rectifier box was bolted to the back of the air filter box so it sits in the battery tray.

shell out for a new loom, or rather two looms as the Commando from 1971 had a separate loom for the headlamp.

I had already bought a solid state rectifier/regulator with the Sparx alternator, as well as a Sparx electronic ignition kit that included the two coils. Before I fitted the harness, I fitted the coils to the bike using a neat little U-shaped bracket located under the nose of the fuel tank, and the bracket was held onto a cross member by four nuts and bolts. I had salvaged the bracket and resprayed it using black Smoothite. While it still bore the scars of the bike's damp history, it was perfectly serviceable. Once I'd bolted it back onto the bike, I fitted the coils and then tried to fit the two front reflectors, but there was not enough room since the coil brackets were in the way. So I had to remove the bracket and that meant removing one of the coils. This was a typical mistake, and a two-minute job had turned into a twenty-minute one as I had not thought it through.

After that I roughly positioned the main loom on the frame by identifying the main connec-

tions, such as the battery leads and coil connections. I inserted the headlamp harness in to the headlamp (this one was a bit more obvious) and it was almost time to connect the two harnesses and the handlebar switches together: but first I needed to sort out the handlebar switches.

I was using original Lucas units. Over the years I have amassed a fair collection of these units from Nortons and Triumphs. I had built up a left-hand side dip/main, horn and headlight flash unit and a right-hand side indicator unit and fitted them to the hi-rider bars, making sure that I had long enough leads from the units to the frame. The two switch harnesses and the headlamp harness connect into the main harness just behind the headstock and this really was spaghetti junction. Luckily Lucas wiring colours were adopted by Triumph and Norton, so the looms from the switches matched the Norton wiring diagram. The first task after connecting was to test that the lights and indicators were working. I could then set up the charging circuit by linking the new alternator to the Sparx regulator/rectifier. This was easy as the three alternator wires connected to the three yellow wires, and then it was just necessary to fix a decent earth with the red wire and connect the black wire to the lead in the main harness that took the DC output from the original rectifier. I bolted the regulator rectifier box to the back of the air filter box, in front of the battery.

A zip tie attached the ignition box to the main frame tube on a rubber pad above the battery compartment, where a neat plug-in loom connected it to the sparky end, and the coils were carefully wired up. The Sparx electronic ignition rotor gubbins was fitted into the points cover, replacing the unserviceable advance/retard unit and the original contact breakers. The two wires from the electronic ignition control box feed into the points compartment through a hole in the back of the timing chest, and a good hint here was to feed the two wires into the points chamber and then solder on the two connectors. I also fitted shrink wrap to the two wires where they run up from the timing case to the frame top tube to tidy them up. I did have a slight problem with a lack of sparks when I came to start the bike. After a certain amount of diagnostic work, including testing the ignition black box on another bike, I traced the fault to the earth connection between the coils and the frame. The powder coating had made an excellent insulator, despite me scraping some off when I made the final connection. With a bit more powder coating removed, sparks were found.

Paint and Finishing

The other job was to get some paint onto the pair of steel side panels I had bought on eBay. I was keen to develop my painting skills and had a couple of aerosol cans of paint made up to match the colour of the fuel tank, which was an orangey red and a close approximation to Tangerine. The best match I could find was a Malagatti colour Rosso Red.

My spraying facilities were limited and I turned to the Mark 2 spray booth – a bigger storage box, again with a hook made from bits of bent coat hanger. Both side panels were given a couple of coats of primer followed by a good few colour coats. All this was done over the New Year break, when it was perishingly cold outside and I had to use a radiator in the garage to keep warm. When painting using aerosols I aim to get the colour on in three or four thin coats, leaving a few minutes between spraying each coat, and then leave the panels to dry for a couple of hours. I then repeat the process, putting on another three or four thin coats of colour and then leaving it to dry overnight. If there are a few runs or sags then on the following day I use 400 wet and dry to flat them off, then 1200 grade to finish the paint off, followed by cutting paste (I use Autoglym Cutting Polish) to get a bit of a shine. The panels were left in the warm for a week to let the paint dry properly, before applying the gold stick-on 'Commando 750' decals and clear lacquer. The job was then complete.

The last couple of jobs were to fix on the new silencers (the exhaust pipes had already been put in place when I fitted the head) and fit the fuel tank. The latter task required a bit of thought, some fruitless exploration of various Norton

The side panel were sprayed using aerosol cans. The stick-on gold 'Commando 750' decals complement the Malagatti Rosso Red.

parts lists, a pair of redundant studs, loads of Norton tank mounting rubber disks, two 3in long studs and a pair of 1970 Bonneville fuel tank mounting rubber top hats. The steel Hi-Rider tank needed a pair of long studs to fit into the holes at the top of the two 'towers' welded to its base, then a big washer, a number of Norton rubber disks to get the right clearance and tank height, then the Triumph top hat rubber to mount the whole lot securely onto the frame cross-member. The rear mount was easy: a thin rubber pad on the frame and a rubber band around the frame that hooked on to two knobs on the back of the tank. With the Hi-Rider seat fitted on the top shock absorber mounts, and the sissy bar that came with the bike bolted firmly to the rear seat tube, the bike was finished.

The following Saturday I primed the crankcases by pumping oil into the hole for the rocker feed pipe on the timing cover, as recommended in the manual. I dragged the bike out of the garage, refitted the fuel tank, added a gallon of Super Unleaded petrol and got the fire extinguisher ready. She fired up on the third kick. A healthy flow of oil was returning to the tank and the bike sounded good with no clunks or rumblings.

There were a few things wrong. The ignition was obviously a bit retarded as the exhaust pipes instantly turned a nice straw colour and the carbs obviously needed some adjusting. The charging light did not light when the ignition was turned on, but glowed healthily (or in fact unhealthily) when the engine was revved. An ammeter made from the two parts of a standard fuse holder on the terminals, fixed inline with the battery, showed that the battery was not charging. So a little bit of fettling was needed. Changing the output wire from the Sparx regulator rectifier to the correct wire in the wiring harness fixed the charging, and strobing the ignition timing made her run smoothly. And that was that – a successful restoration.

The Commando completed, pictured by the statue of the Duke of Wellington at Aldershot.

The drive side of the Hi-Rider looks lean, and the author likes the high bars and chopper-style seat.

Registering the Bike

In order to get the bike registered in the UK, and therefore able to be ridden on the road, there were a few more hurdles to leap. As the bike was a historic vehicle, I could apply for an age related number plate and to do that I had to go to the UK Driver and Vehicle Licensing Agency (DVLA). In the UK a vehicle manufactured before January 1973 is eligible for the 'historic' class for vehicle excise duty, which means there is no yearly fee to tax the vehicle. In order to apply for a 'new' registration document, there is a set of data that needs to be supplied to the DVLA. The main form needed is the V55/5, which, to quote the DVLA:

> ... is used by Independent dealers, Import dealers and individuals to register brand new vehicles, new and used imported vehicles, kit built vehicles, rebuilt vehicles and used vehicles not previously registered at DVLA.

A new registration number will only be issued to a roadworthy vehicle, as the registration process includes the issue of a Road Fund Licence or tax disc. In order to get a tax disc, you must have a valid MOT test certificate and insurance, so you have to get the bike ready for the road before it can be registered.

The V55/5 form is available from the DVLA and local offices, or you can request a form to be posted by ringing the DVLA (0870 240 0010) and eventually getting through to a human after a convoluted time working through their automated call system. The form identifies the additional information that needs to be provided.

In order to get a historic registration number, a range of supporting information and data is needed to support the application. As well as the V55/5 application form, I needed:

Dating certificate. The dating certificate provides the DVLA with the date of manufacture of the vehicle from an independent and approved source. The Norton Owners Club, of which I am a member, provided me with a certificate. Rubbings of the frame and engine numbers and photographs of the finished bike were needed before a certificate could be issued. If the bike is an import from the USA and has US title documents, the DVLA will accept the date of manufacture as documented on the US Title document.

MOT certificate. Once the restoration is complete the bike must be MOT tested to ensure it is roadworthy before a registration number and tax disc is issued. I trailered the bike to the MOT test.

Insurance. As stated above, you will need to get the bike insured before applying for a registration number. Since a registration number has not yet been issued, the bike needs to be insured on the basis of the frame number, and this did not pose a problem with my insurer. Once you get a registration number, the insurer must be told so the cover can be updated.

Identification documents. In order to register a machine, you must provide evidence of your identification. A photocard driving licence is acceptable, but if you don't have one, then you must provide proof of your identity (an old-style paper licence, passport, marriage certificate, decree nisi/absolute certificate or birth certificate) and proof of your address as on the V55/5 (one of utility bill, bank/building society statement, medical card or Council Tax bill for the current year).

You have to pay a fee for the registration and to cover the cost of the Road Fund Licence. As the Norton was originally built before 1973, its Tax Class was 'Historic Vehicle', so the Road Fund Licence fee was zero. The registration fee in March 2010 was £55.

Once I had assembled all the evidence and filled in V55/5, I took the paperwork to my DVLA local office. The vast majority of boxes in the V55/5 are irrelevant to a historic vehicle and those I was unsure about had been left blank. I presented the V55/5 and the supporting evidence (including the fee) and hoped they would issue me with an age-related number directly. The office staff verified my identification using my photocard driving licence and then that the V55/5 was filled in and the supporting evidence was correct. They took the V55/5, MOT certificate, dating certificate, insurance certificate and the £55 fee, issued me with a tracking reference number and told me that I would get a reply soon. A couple of days later a letter arrived saying that the bike needed to be inspected. The letter contained details of the time and place for the inspection, which turned out to be four weeks later at a VOSA testing station about 25 miles from home. Usefully they included a map. The instructions emphasized that the bike could not be ridden to the inspection, so on the appointed day I hitched up the trailer and drove the bike over to the testing station.

Once there the DVLA inspector examined the bike, checking the frame and engine numbers and verifying that they matched those on the V55/5. He also looked at the receipt I had received from the original vendor and some of the receipts from various parts suppliers. After a chat about the restoration and spares availability, the inspector seemed happy and told me they would be in touch. Altogether the inspection process took about fifteen minutes.

Nine days later all of my documents were returned from the local office, along with a new tax disc and a 'Number Plate Authorisation Certificate' (DVLA Form V948). The covering letter stated that a new V5C would be sent to me from DVLA in the next four weeks. I was able to get a registration number plate made up using the V948. After giving the new registration number to the bike's insurer, I was at last able to ride the bike on the road.

The new V5C logbook arrived in the post between four and five weeks later, completing the process.

Bibliography and Further Reading

Bacon, Roy, *Norton Twin Restoration* (Niton Publishing, 2000). A restoration guide to all the Norton vertical twins, including the Commando, with lots of contemporary photos and detailed specifications.

Bacon, Roy, *Norton Twins: The Postwar 500, 600, 650, 750, 850 and Lightweight Twins* (Niton Publishing, 1995). Comprehensive guide to all the postwar Norton twins.

Clarke, R. M., *Norton Commando Gold Portfolio* (Booklands Books, 1995). A collection of road tests and technical articles from the contemporary UK, US and Australian motorcycle press. An excellent source of original information on the Commando.

Clew, Jeff, *Norton Commando Super Profile* (J. T. Foulis and Co. Ltd, 1983). The Super Profile series provides a brief history of the subject, contemporary road tests and riders' impressions of the subject, along with excellent photography showing details of the bike.

Duckworth, Mick, *Norton Commando* (Haynes Publishing, 2004). Good history of the Commando.

Frick, Michael, ed., *Tech Digest* (International Norton Owners Association, 1999). This is a collection of technical hints and tips aimed mainly at the Commando, but covering some earlier Nortons. It is available from the UK Norton Owners Club.

Hopwood, Bert, *Whatever Happened to the British Motorcycle Industry?* (Haynes Publishing, 1981). The definitive account of the post-Second World War decline of the industry, told through the eyes of the designer of the Norton Twin engine.

Magrath, Derek, *Norton: The Complete Story* (Crowood Press, 1997). A comprehensive history of the Norton Company from its earliest days to 1990.

Shilton, Neil, *A Million Miles Ago* (Haynes Publishing,1982). A fine account of one man's work in the British motorcycle industry, with specific details on the development of the Triumph Saint and Norton Interpol models.

Stevens, Tim, and John Hudson, *NOC Commando Service Notes*, ed. Alan Osborn (Norton Owners Club, 1979). This publication gives details of improvements and modifications that can be made to the Commande and is an excellent record of owners' experiences of improvements. It is no longer in print and I sourced my copy from eBay.

Wilson, Steve, *British Motor Cycles since 1950, volume 3* (Patrick Stephens Limited: ISBN 0-85059-626-2). Excellent history of Norton and all the bikes produced since 1950, including the Commando. Especially useful are the comprehensive details of the final years of NVT.

www.nortonownersclub.org. The Norton Owners Club provides technical advice, dating letters, and social runs, rallies and meets for Norton owners.

Two very useful Internet resources I have used are *RealClassic* (www.realclassic.co.uk) and the Jerry Doe Norton Commando site (www.jerrydoe.com), both of which provided me with support and technical advice while writing this book.

Recommended Suppliers

All of the suppliers listed below provided spares, service or advice to me during the rebuild. I can thoroughly recommend them both in terms of the quality of goods supplied and the service provided. All the suppliers are UK based (unless otherwise stated) and the telephone numbers are for the UK (international callers should replace the first 0 with 44).

Andover Norton International Ltd
3 Old Farm Buildings, Standen Manor Estate, Hungerford, Berkshire RG17 0RB
Tel.: 01488 686816   Fax: 01488 686826
www.andover-norton.co.uk
Email: office@andover-norton.com
Genuine Norton spares from the original factory drawings, supplied to both the trade and the public.

Central Wheel Components Ltd
Wheel House, 8 & 9 Station Road, Coleshill, Birmingham B46 1HT
Tel.: 01675 462264   Fax: 01675 466412
www.central-wheel.co.uk
Email: info@central-wheel.co.uk
Suppliers of rims and spokes. I have used this supplier for all my restorations and have always received prompt and knowledgeable service. Rims and spokes have always been of good quality, with a range of options such as 'ordinary' and 'better' quality chrome rims, alloy rims and stainless steel rims. They also supply tyres and will build wheels.

www.ebay.co.uk
Ebay is a wonderful source of both spares and literature relating to classic bikes, and indeed classic bikes as well. It's an autojumble online where you can search for the parts you need, but be careful – if something looks too good to be true, then it probably is.

www.feked.com
Tel.: 0845 5190620
Email: info@feked.com
This company is a supplier of classic motorcycle parts and has a good online shop that is easy to use and goods are dispatched quickly. The exhaust pipes and silencers I bought from there were good quality, and they fitted straight out of the box.

Hart Motorcycle Services
Redfields Stables, Redfields Lane, Church Crookham, Hants GU52 0RB
Tel.: 01252 851037
While not stocking specific Triumph spares, they do carry oil and general spares such as batteries, carburettor fittings, cable nipples, tyres and inner tubes. They also do number plates, mechanical work and MoT tests.

Mick Hemmings Motorcycles
72–74 Overstone Road, Northampton NN1 3JS
Tel.: 01604 638505
www.mickhemmings.com
A long-established Norton specialist with a good reputation for quality parts.

Motor Sport Coatings
Unit 5, Icknield Road, Ipsden, Wallingford, Oxfordshire OX10 6AS
Tel.: 01491 875699
Email: mikehodges@supanet.com

MSC shot-blasted and repaired my frame, vapour-blasted the engine and primary chain cases, welded up a crack in the chain case and powder-coated the frame and engine mounts. All the work was done to a very high standard and in the estimated time. Recommended.

Norvil Motorcycle Company

The Corner Garage, 96–98 Cannock Road, Chase Terrace, Burntwood, Staffordshire WS7 1JP
Tel.: 01543 278008
www.norvilmotorcycle.co.uk.
Norvil supplied many parts by mail order and always delivered quickly. They provide an excellent catalogue and hold lots of stock parts. The quality was excellent, everything fitted and they also offer a useful technical support line.

PJS Polishing Ltd

4 Vulcan Way, Swan Lane, Sandhurst, Berks GU47 9DB
Tel.: 07747 028944   Fax: 01252 872209
Peter Sturgeon provided an excellent service and sorted out the chroming of my footrest hangers and brake pedal.

RGM Motors

Halle Bank Farm, Beckermet, Cumbria CA21 2XB
Tel.: 01946 841517
www.rgmmotors.co.uk
Norton specialists who produce an excellent catalogue, have good stocks and dispatch parts quickly. They provided a large number of spares during the rebuild.

Rockerbox

31 The Street, Wrecclesham, Farnham, Surrey GU10 4QS
Tel.: 01252 722973
Support your local motorcycle shop! Mainly Triumph spares but some Norton, and lots of 'supporting' parts, such as Lucas and Amal, and mechanical work. Get advice from Darrell, spannering by Arthur, tea by request.

Roe Engineering (Fleet) Ltd

10 Kings Road, Fleet, Hants GU51 3AD
Tel.: 01252 613404
Roe Engineering carried out various engineering tasks on my rebuild, including the rebore, crank re-grind, releasing the pistons and removing the old spark plugs, all to a high standard and at reasonable cost.

Speedo Repairs

Tel.: 01252 329826, 07824 884434
www.speedorepairs.co.uk
Email: enquiries@speedorepairs.co.uk
I have used north-west Surrey-based Speedo Repairs for some years for all my Smiths speedo and tacho repairs and refurbishments, both magnetic and chronometric. The proprietor, Ashley Pople, has always done a good job, but is very busy so it can take him a few weeks to turn repairs around.

Tri-Cor

The Old Hopkiln, Whitwick Manor, Lower Eggleton, Ledbury, Herefordshire HR8 2UE
Tel. and Fax: 01432 820752
www.tri-corengland.com
Email: sales@tri-corengland.com
Tri-Cor (formerly Rare Spares) has consistently provided excellent service and quality goods for many years. Orders have always been dispatched promptly and contained what I had ordered. Tri-Cor also runs Sparx, who manufacture various electrical components, including alternators and stators, various rectifiers and regulator 'black boxes', Lucas-style switchgear and electronic ignition kits.

Vehicle Wiring Products

9 Buxton Court, Manners Industrial Estate, Ilkeston, Derbyshire DE7 8EF
Tel.: 01159 305454   Fax: 0115 9440101
Email: sales@vehicleproducts.co.uk
Suppliers of everything you need to rewire a bike, such as bullet connectors, spade terminals and correctly colour-coded wire. They also do reproduction switches, lights, indicators and electrical fixtures, and other motorcycle-related items such as control levers. I have received consistently good service from this firm on all my restorations.

Index

Etta's Baby Lamb

written by Jay Dale

illustrated by Jacqueline East

Etta looked out of the window.
She could see Dad coming up the road.
He was carrying something
small and white.
Etta ran out of the house
and down the road to Dad.

"Dad!" called Etta.
"What have you got there?"

"It's a baby lamb," said Dad.
"This poor little lamb
doesn't have a mother.
We'll have to take care of him."

3

"Oh, you poor little thing," said Etta.
"Can I help you take care of him, Dad?"

"Yes!" smiled Dad.
"You can take care of him every day."

Dad took the baby lamb onto the decking.
"Sit down here," said Dad to Etta.
"You can hold the baby lamb
while I get him some sheep's milk."

Etta sat down on an old chair.
Dad placed the baby lamb
carefully in her arms.
The lamb felt warm and soft.

"I won't be long," said Dad,
and he quickly went to get the milk.
Etta patted the baby lamb's ears
and rubbed him under the chin.

"Baaaa! Baaaa!" cried the baby lamb.
"Dad won't be long," Etta whispered softly.

Just then, Dad came back
with a bottle of warm milk.
He passed the milk to Etta.
"What should I do?" asked Etta.

"Just hold the top of the bottle
up to the lamb's mouth," said Dad.
"He should start to drink."

Etta held the bottle
up to the lamb's mouth.
The baby lamb quickly began to drink.

"Oh!" cried Etta.
"This baby lamb is very hungry."

"Yes," smiled Dad.
"You will need to feed him every day.
You can feed him a bottle of milk in
the morning and a bottle of milk at night.
Do you think you can do that?"

"Yes!" smiled Etta.
"I **can** do that!"

"Great," said Dad.
"I'll feed him during the day."

As the last of the milk went
from the bottle, the little lamb's eyes
began to close.
"Our little lamb is sleepy," said Dad.
"We need to find him a cozy bed."

"But first," smiled Etta,
"we need to give him a name."

"Yes!" said Dad.
"What would you like to call him, Etta?"

Etta patted the lamb's ears again
and tickled him under the chin.
"Well," said Etta,
"he does have one white ear
and one ear with a little brown spot.
I think we should call him Spot."

Just then Spot's eyes closed shut.

"He's fast asleep," whispered Etta.

"But he can't sleep on my lap all day."

Dad just laughed.

"Come on," he grinned, "I have an idea."

Dad gently lifted Spot from Etta's lap

and carried him to the end of the deck.

"I think this old kennel

will do just fine," said Dad.

"It will be big enough for a little lamb."

13

Etta raced inside the house
and got an old blanket.
She placed it inside the kennel.
Then Dad put Spot
gently into the kennel.
Spot's eyes didn't open at all.
He was still fast asleep!

"Spot should be safe here," said Dad.
"But later today we will make
him a pen and put the kennel in there."

Etta bent down and patted
Spot's little brown ear.
"Sleep well my baby lamb," she whispered.
"We'll take good care of you."